THE POWER
OF YOUR
PERCEPTIONS

POTENTIALS
GUIDES FOR PRODUCTIVE LIVING

Wayne E. Oates, General Editor

THE POWER
OF YOUR
PERCEPTIONS

by

WILLIAM V. ARNOLD

THE WESTMINSTER PRESS
Philadelphia

Scripture quotations from the Revised Standard Version of the Bible are copyrighted 1946, 1952, © 1971, 1973 by the Division of Christian Education of the National Council of the Churches of Christ in the U.S.A., and are used by permission.

Book Design by Alice Derr

First edition

Published by The Westminster Press ®
Philadelphia, Pennsylvania

PRINTED IN THE UNITED STATES OF AMERICA
9 8 7 6 5 4 3 2 1

Library of Congress Cataloging in Publication Data

Arnold, William V., 1941–
    The power of your perceptions.

    (Potentials)
    Bibliography: p.
    1. Perception. 2. Christian life—1960–
I. Title. II. Series.
BF311.A723 1984   248.4   83-26089
ISBN 0-664-24524-2 (pbk.)

To
Kathy

Contents

Foreword

The eleven books in this series, Potentials: Guides for Productive Living, speak to your condition and mine in the life we have to live today. The books are designed to ferret out the potentials you have with which to rise above rampant social and psychological problems faced by large numbers of individuals and groups. The purpose of rising above the problems is portrayed as far more than merely your own survival, merely coping, and merely "succeeding" while others fail. These books with one voice encourage you to save your own life by living with commitment to Jesus Christ, and to be a creative servant of the common good as well as your own good.

In this sense, the books are handbooks of ministry with a new emphasis: coupling your own well-being with the well-being of your neighbor. You use the tools of comfort wherewith God comforts you to be a source of strength to those around you. A conscious effort has been made by each author to keep these two dimensions of the second great commandment of our Lord Jesus Christ in harmony with each other.

The two great commandments are summarized in Luke 10:25–28: "And behold, a lawyer stood up to put him to the test, saying, 'Teacher, what shall I do to inherit eternal life?' He said to him, 'What is written in the law? How do you read?' And he answered, 'You shall love the Lord your God with all your heart, and with all your soul, and with all your strength, and with all your mind; and your neighbor as yourself.' And he said to him, 'You have answered right; do this, and you will live.' "

Underneath the two dimensions of neighbor and self there is also a persistent theme: The only way you can receive such harmony of thought and action is by the intentional re-centering of your life on the sovereignty of God and the rapid rejection of all idols that would enslave you. The theme, then, of this series of books is that these words of Jesus are the master guides both to the realization of your own potentials and to productive living in the nitty-gritty of your day's work.

The books in this series are unique, and each claims your attention separately in several ways.

First, these books address great social issues of our day, but they do so in terms of your own personal involvement in and responses to the problems. For example, the general problem of the public school system, the waste in American consumer-ism, the health hazards in a lack of rest and vocational burnout, the crippling effects of a defective mental outlook, and the incursion of Eastern mystical traditions into Western Christian activism are all larger-than-life issues. Yet each author translates the problem into the terms of day-to-day living and gives concrete guidelines as to what you can do about the problem.

Second, these books address the undercurrent of helpless-ness that overwhelming epidemic problems produce in you. The authors visualize you throwing up your hands and saying: "There is nothing *anyone* can do about it." Then they show you that this is not so, and that there are things *you* can do about it.

Third, the authors have all disciplined themselves to stay off their own soapboxes and to limit oratory about how awful the world is. They refuse to stop at gloomy diagnoses of incurable conditions. They go on to deal with your potentials for changing yourself and your world in very specific ways. They do not let you, the reader, off the hook with vague, global utterances and generalized sermons. They energize you with a sense of hope that is generated by basic information, clear decision-making, and new directions taken by you yourself.

Fourth, these books get their basic interpretations and recommendations from a careful plumbing of the depths of the power of faith in God through Jesus Christ. They are not books that leave you with the illusion that you can lift yourself and your world by pulling hard at your own bootstraps. They energize and inspire you through the hope and strength that God in Christ is making available to you through the wisdom of the Bible and the presence of the living Christ in your life. Not even this, though, is presented in a namby-pamby or trite way. You will be surprised with joy at the freshness of the applications of biblical truths which you have looked at so often that you no longer notice their meaning. You will do many "double takes" with reference to your Bible as you read these books. You will find that the Bread of Life is not too holy or too good for human nature's daily food.

William Arnold is Dean of the Faculty and Professor of Pastoral Care and Counseling at Union Theological Seminary in Richmond, Virginia. He has written this book to enable you to stand back a few steps and assess carefully how you yourself look at or perceive your world, your relationships to other people, and your self. All of these are objective, out-there realities which you *choose* to perceive, interpret, and understand in your own particular ways. The *choices* you make are yours and, once made, shape your behavior, condition your personal happiness, and create your outlook on life. In a very real way, your perceptions have differing depths until they become ingrained *beliefs* of yours. As such, perceptions are powerful, but not more powerful than you are to change them through learning, discipline, conversation with others, and prayer before God. You live within the bounds of your perceptions, and yet within those bounds you are not without the power to learn, grow, and redirect your own life through God's revelation of the changes that you with God's help can make in your perceptions.

William Arnold cautions us against the fallacies of much self-help literature that misleads us into thinking that we can ignore our creatureliness and the roots of life. He leads us carefully through a psychological and social understanding of how our perceptions work in dealing with our feelings of sadness, disappointment, and fear; he also emphasizes the way faulty perceptions distort and mix up our communication with those we love. He underscores the gifts we have to offer through the wisdom of accurate perceptions or understandings.

The whole substance of reworking your perception of your world, self, and neighbor is summed up in exchanging bad judgment for good sense, building your beliefs upon facts rather than fancies, hearing what people actually are saying instead of following your bias as to what you assume they mean, learning to say what you feel accurately—all of which add up to sound common sense.

Then Arnold devotes two chapters to tackling two of the most common sufferings that can be dealt with through exercising the power of your perceptions: depression and stress. You will find the practical wisdom revealing that you are not helpless in the face of these aching necessities of life.

In the final chapter Arnold sets the whole psychological and social concern with accurate perception in the biblical context of God's intention and comfort in the sweaty process of "thinking God's thoughts after him" and gaining God's perspectives for our lives. You are about to read a guidebook for getting an understanding heart.

WAYNE E. OATES

Louisville, Kentucky

Introduction

If I step into the street and hear a loud roar followed by a screeching noise, my brain quickly interprets all those signals to mean that a car is about to hit me. My understanding of the world tells me that my body is not likely to withstand the inpact of that mass of metal. Furthermore, I believe that my life is worth saving. All of those processes are involved in perception, the term we use to describe how we understand, or believe, what the world *is*. A dictionary definition helps us to understand that perception is the act or faculty of forming a picture of ourselves and the world by means of the senses or of the mind. In short, perception is the act of putting information together and interpreting it so that we can use it as a blueprint for action. Information is taken in, interpreted, evaluated, and converted into a decision to be acted upon. So I jump! If I were deeply depressed or intoxicated, those factors would alter my perception. My interpretation of what was taking place could then result in a very different response on my part.

The above example is relatively simple. Perception can be far more complex. Consider this: A husband and wife have been married for forty years. In raising three children, they have shared values in how to educate and rear them. In their perception, raising children has been the major purpose in marriage. The children are now long gone. The husband comes home later and later. The wife spends long periods of time in front of the television set. Conversation is sparse. Depression sets in. Neither understands what is wrong. There has been no affair, no flagrant violation of their marriage vows. Yet they *perceive* that something has left their marriage. No explanations or alternatives seem clear. Their interpretation, or understanding, of marriage did not deal with the question of what happens after the children are gone. There's nothing left to do, as it were. Perception is the powerful force here. The way their world is now doesn't fit into what they were prepared for. Neither does their world of perception contain strategies for action when new situations develop, as when children are not around. If their perception is not dealt with, things in their world probably will continue to deteriorate.

Your perception of the world is the subject of this book. You carry around interpretations about your world. Those interpretations influence the choices you make about what to do and how to feel. We can see evidence of the influence of perception in all sorts of common occurrences. Two women lose their husbands by death. One collapses, vows that without her husband "life is not worth living" (a perception), and winds up in a long-term psychiatric facility. The other grieves openly and, when asked how she will go on, says, "I know that God never places more on us than we are able to bear." We may find that we are not in agreement with either of those perceptions of how the world and God operate. Nonetheless, they are very different perceptions that are quite influential in the response that each of these women makes to life and the future.

Writers exploit the issue regularly. Large numbers of self-help volumes share a common desire to enable you to perceive the world in a particular way. Suggestions are given about how to process the information that bombards you from the world, how to interpret and respond to the myriads of situations with which you deal. After all, the interpretation you make pretty well determines your response.

Consider these common phrases, slogans, and statements of belief:

> "What you see is what you get."
> "God never places more on us than we are able to withstand."
> "A self-fulfilling prophecy."
> "All you have to do is believe."
> "Faith can move mountains."

These phrases and others flow daily from our lips as we attempt to negotiate the tasks of living. They reveal our *perceptions* of the world. Further, they dictate, more or less, the way in which we will respond to that world which we perceive. The secret is that you and I *form* these perceptions. We have *chosen* them, even though we may not realize it, with the miraculous ability that God has given us.

The fascinating—and frustrating—thing about perception is that we don't all agree on what the world is like. Our perceptions are not the same, and thus our responses to the world are not the same. What explanation is there for these differing perceptions that result in such variety? And what control do you have, if any, over your perceptions of the world? The answers to these questions hold great importance for your experience of well-being and for the relationships you hold most dear.

The word "perceive" appears frequently in the Bible. References to Jesus and statements made by him give us deeper insight into the importance of perception. Far more than just seeing, the word carries a note of going far beneath the surface to find "what is" and "what can be." As we seek to understand more about perception, we shall attempt to take grateful advantage of God's grace in Jesus Christ. And we shall attempt to avoid falling too easily into the camp of those who "hear but never understand, and . . . see but never perceive" (Matt. 13:14).

This book attempts to examine perception and its power. We will be conducting our examination from an admittedly Christian perspective. Nonetheless, our Christian viewpoint openly and warmly receives, and is aided by, information from other helping and scientific disciplines.

Theologically, we will be dealing with what it means to be human. And that is our beginning point.

Part I

UNDERSTANDING YOUR PERCEPTIONS

Chapter 1

Your Perception
of Yourself
Before God

In order to understand perception, let's discuss who on earth and before God we think we are. That, of course, is a perception in itself. What we are really talking about is who we *believe* ourselves to be! What are some of the characteristics you and I share, as perceived in the Christian tradition? Later, we will begin to talk about how these perceptions shape our responses to ourselves and the world around us.

We are finite creatures. Human beings are limited creatures. That is what being "finite" means. It is a traditional formulation in a "doctrine of humankind," and there is nothing very profound about it. We are born; we grow, mature, and age; we are limited by time and space; we die. That is easy to see, but we resist it with all our might.

Put very simply, we are unable to know everything, and we are unable to be or become all that we would like to be. A very wise teacher, Jürgen Moltmann, says that we are biologically *defective* creatures. The primary characteristic of this defectiveness in us is that we are "open to the world without a protective environment, overstimulated by signals from the external world and uncertain in . . . instincts. . . . Nature has left [us] a comparatively incomplete animal" (*Man,* p. 5). Moltmann compares our human life with the life of animals.

Other animals seem to have a specialized understanding of the world and their place in it. They respond more uniformly and predictably than you or I. Our finiteness shows up in our lack of understanding about who we are and what our purpose is. From the very first we have the added job of joining together with each other and with God to figure out who we are and what we're supposed to be up to. Not being able to agree with each other about that is a major limitation! Our beginning is very uncertain, with few clear directions.

Part of our limitation is that we cannot even take in all the signals that come to us from the world. We cannot hear all the sounds. For instance, dogs have a capacity to hear sounds that we cannot hear. The color spectrum is not fully available to us because of the limitations of our visual senses. Science fascinates us as discoveries are made of things we never knew existed.

Not only are there chunks and globs of information that are not available to human beings generally; each one of us has unique possibilities and variations for what information we take in. Some of us are blind, others deaf; some have perfect pitch, others an acute sense of smell. Most of us have more moderate differences. But each of them limits as well as helps us.

The overstimulation of signals that we *can* receive demonstrates that we cannot possibly organize all of them, especially not all by ourselves. This is another limitation. Thus we begin to pick and choose information, resulting in very different perceptions of the world. "Did you see how angry that clerk was at the grocery store?" says one person. "I thought she was very efficient," replies the second. "Didn't you see how intense she was about keeping the line moving?" They both "saw" the same person. They both "saw" very different things. Those different perceptions are a result, in part, of the limited spectrum of information that each had selected—without thinking much about it. It happens every day. Our limitations show up in the selected number of signals we attend to *and* the principles of interpretation that we have adopted.

Perception concerns the information you take in at any given moment and the way you organize that information into some kind of pattern or whole. Your interpretation comes from quite different experiences out of other times and places. Those experiences also limit you. Consider the culture shock of persons moving into a new environment. Customs differ, relationships are handled differently. Looking a person in the eye is a sign of trust in our culture, but an invasion of personal space in another. Acceptance into a group depends on shared perceptions. The new persons who don't "know" are limited by previous experience. There are no instincts that determine what those persons should do. A new process begins that builds up a new perception of who they are and how they may be able to fit into this new culture.

Stress, which is a popular word these days, is itself a neutral word. But nowadays, when a person speaks of being "stressed," she or he usually means "overloaded." There is too much to do, too much information to take in, too much to organize. A person just can't do it, and the body objects to being asked to exceed its capabilities.

One of the most difficult things for many people to do is to acknowledge what they *can't* do. Yet that is the affirmation we are called to make about ourselves from a Christian perspective. I envy the people who can say: "No, I can't do that. I have taken on all that I can handle already." They are very sound and show that they know how God created them. They *perceive* their limits and respond appropriately. I sometimes have to go back and get out of obligations because of my inability to acknowledge my limits in the first place. Finitude catches up with me. It overrules my perception that a few more hours and days could be squeezed out of my existence for a project that is so worthwhile. What a relief when that realization of limits comes! It is a new perception. I can take a deep breath and give thanks for the very Judeo-Christian affirmation that allows me to be me, and that it does not encourage me to pursue my *super*human illusions.

Yes, we are limited. God has set our boundaries. We discover them in prayer with God and in fellowship with each other. And that perception will help us in times of suffering, stress, and temptation. Later in this book, we will deal with more practical ways of taking advantage of that perception. Right now, let us acknowledge the reality of being limited in what we can attempt to do at one time. Instead of trying to do everything at once, as a nonfinite creature would be able to do, we have to move along in an orderly manner. *Organization* is a way of handling multiple needs when we have a limited amount of things we can process at any one time. Organization gives the promise that we will get to it eventually, if we limit the amount we take on in any given moment. You and I are, with God's help, the organizers.

We are tempted to deny our finitude. We won't settle for accepting limits. Rather, we proceed to convince ourselves otherwise. Often we have described this in Christian theology as sin. Sin is, among other things, the act of distorting the truth about ourselves. Denying my finitude, convincing myself that I can do anything, is, in this sense, sin. We pay the price over and over again for such distortion. Some bodily symptoms and disorders quite properly might be described as consequences of sin. Gastric distress and headaches can often be explained in terms of the limits we exceeded earlier. God is not punishing us; we are, in fact, punishing ourselves for not acknowledging our limitations. We asked for it; we got it. "What you see is what you get."

A frequent question asked by seriously ill people is, "Pastor, what could I have done that God would punish me like this?" I do not believe that God punishes such persons for some grievous sin. But I do believe that it is important for us to explore the way these persons have viewed themselves and how they have pushed the limits. It *may* be that these persons are paying the price for pushing too hard, for denying the limits of the body and the psyche, for ignoring their humanity.

Remember the importance of watching out for distorted perception—interpretations of the world that lead us to behave in self-defeating ways. Correction of the distortion is needed in order to provide sanctuary, stability, and clear vision. We will look for ways to clear up these vision problems.

We do tend to distort things toward what we perceive to be our own best interests. Communication is very difficult for that very reason. Scott Peck, in his helpful book *The Road Less Traveled*, describes one evening's chess game with his nine-year-old daughter. His intention was to have a good, constructive, relationship-building time with her. As the evening wore on, her bedtime approached. But Dr. Peck was winning. He urged her to stay up past her bedtime so they could finish the game. After a while, she jumped up and dashed off to her room, crying. He realized the distortion that had taken place. His original intention of strengthening a relationship had been distorted by the perception that he was winning. The power of that perception, that desire to win, had overrun the importance of his original goal. Sinful? Yes, in the sense that distortion damaged (temporarily) a more important hope.

Forgivable? Yes! Before God we can laugh at our mispercep-
tions and feel loved by God in spite of them.

Distortion takes place regularly in our lives. A perception
of ourselves that takes distortion into account helps us guard
against some of the harm that can come from it.

Notice that this discussion of distortion moved inevitably
into a discussion of relationships. And that is the next
characteristic of our perceptions of ourselves before God.

*We are made for and in need of relationships with other human
beings.* This perception is expressed in many different ways.
Scripture places much importance on the community of faith.
The church concretely expresses that conviction.

Karl Barth writes: "Humanity, the characteristic and essential mode of man's being, is in its root fellow-humanity.
Humanity which is not fellow-humanity is inhumanity"
(*Church Dogmatics,* Vol. III, Pt. 4, p. 117). If we are not in
relationship to meaningful other people, we have limited our
capacity to be human. Partnerships of one kind or another are
part of the warp and woof of our existence. These partnerships are two-way covenants. Complicated as relationships
may be, we would be less than human if we did not enter into
them. Finitude and distortion come into stark face-to-face
reality in personal relationships. But it is in these relationships as well that we come to terms with the reality of our
limitations and distortions through the gift of the perspective
and perception of another human being. Our community
enables our perceptions to grow, change, adjust, and be
reinterpreted as we learn more and more about ourselves,
each other, and God.

Such a learning process necessarily involves building up
relationships and the perceptions that enable those relationships to maintain themselves. Moltmann describes human
beings as "culture-making creatures" (*Man,* pp. 6–7). Such a

capacity is evidence of the creative possibilities that exist for us. But those possibilities seem to come into being when we, in one way or another, make use of relationships, the community that surrounds us.

Pop music, which constantly revolves around the change and the difference made by a relationship, reflects this fact about ourselves. The major task of maturing for adolescents focuses on the importance of faithfulness in relationships. Many of our difficulties in life reflect the breakdown of significant bonds between persons.

Writers from many walks of life wrestle with this observation about human nature. Hans Selye, for instance, observes that "every living being looks out for itself first of all." But he goes on to observe that "the common denominator of all man's noble or vulgar efforts ... seems to be a striving, consciously or subconsciously, to earn good will and gratitude from one source or another" (in William Glasser, *Stations of the Mind*, p. xvi).

We need each other. In fact, we are prone to need each other in a way that is hard to resist. I remember well the experience of working on a special unit in a psychiatric hospital with patients who had pending criminal charges. Each day when I entered the locked ward, a certain man would run to the other end of the room and then hurl a string of expletives at me. I was frightened and stayed clear of him. Finally, another patient came up to me one day and asked, "Don't you understand that he wants to talk to you?" *That* perception had never entered my mind! Yet it turned out to be true. The only way that man had ever been able to get someone's attention was to do something bizarre. And he couldn't understand why it hadn't worked with me. His solution was to get more bizarre each day. Here is a combination of the human factors we have been describing. He had limited experience, which had led to a distorted perception of how to get in touch with someone. His need for that communication, however, was painfully real, as I discovered over the weeks and months that followed.

You and I are gifted creatures. The picture that has been described thus far is not a bad one. It is simply a statement about who we are. These very characteristics result in a variety of gifts and possibilities. While we may speak of ourselves as limited creatures, we are also creatures who have a seemingly endless list of possibilities. The history of humankind might be summed up as a movement toward expanding our options. Certainly, some options turn out not to be in our best interests, but an impressive list of accomplishments can be built up of constructive gifts to ourselves as the human community. To focus on the destructive results of our history or to focus on only the positive would be the worst of distortions about who we are. We are persons created in the image of God, persons for whom Christ died.

Move with caution before you adopt a fully bad image of yourself. You cannot deny the gifts that seem so plentiful throughout humankind. No one person can take in, appreciate, or use all of them. We must still pick and choose our priorities. We must work to build up a community, a culture, that provides freedom of choice and also that recognizes the dangers that come when such a freedom is extended. Our perceptions about how much to trust human beings with freedom or how much *not* to trust them is the stuff upon which political theories are constructed.

Reexamine, then, your fundamental beliefs about being human. They will keep coming up as we get more and more case material to examine.

Our next task is to ask *how much* control we have over our perceptions of ourselves and the world. How are your perceptions formed in the first place? That calls for some examination of our roots, which will be the focus of the next chapter.

Chapter 2

The Roots
of Your Perceptions

Have you ever gotten into one of those fascinating conversations about babies? One in particular revolves around whether infants have personalities at birth. No doubt you have heard folks speak of the "quiet one." Or perhaps you have heard other folks talk about their child's "crying and refusing to go to sleep from the very first night." If you stick with the conversation long enough, and with people who have older children, stories unfold about how those characteristics hold true as the years pass.

The technical subject of such conversations has to do with genetic influences. Aren't we born with predispositions, behavioral characteristics, and, for our purposes, ways of perceiving things? Many give an affirmative answer to that question. Strong theories of personality are built around that assumption.

Of course, on the other side of the debate are the environmentalists of personality, who hold out for the importance of influences exerted upon us by parents, other significant people, and early experiences. Those who have carried this theory to the extreme often claim that personality is shaped by the age of six. That kind of assertion has terrified many a parent.

The truth, of course, is probably "both/and" rather than "either/or." Persons engaged in genetic research continue to find more and more characteristics that have their origins in the chromosomes. Few of these persons, however, would make the claim that environment does not affect the way in which those characteristics express themselves. Environmentalists also yield.

In this chapter we are going to look at the "givens" that seem to come with us from birth. There have been a number of helpful theories which can contribute to our understanding.

One of the most helpful approaches comes from the work of Carl Jung. One of his most famous works is *Psychological Types,* in which he describes differences among human beings that seem to be givens. With proper appreciation for these typical differences among people, he maintains, we could understand ourselves and others more clearly. An outgrowth of Jung's work has been a personality inventory called the Myers-Briggs Type Indicator.

In large part, Jung's "types" were attempts to help us understand different ways of perceiving things. Another way of describing perception, you will remember, is in terms of what we pay attention to. According to Jung, we have the capacity to pay attention to many things; however, there are certain areas of the world and ourselves to which we pay attention *first.* For instance, Jung speaks of extraversion and introversion. Because of our popular understanding of those words, I'm going to try to use different language to talk about these ways of perceiving.

World First/Me First?

One of these types describes me very well. I am a person who tends to look outside myself first, particularly when I am wrestling with a problem or when I am fatigued or troubled. Those of us who look to the world first have some character-istics that are humorous at times and painful at other times. We think out loud, for example. A tongue-in-cheek way of describing this characteristic cautions people not to believe the first thing that we say, because we've just started to think! What really happens is that we conduct our processes of thinking out loud. In fact, interaction with other people aids our thinking. Furthermore, we probably learn things better through conversation and interaction with other people. After all, since our tendency is to turn to the world first, it is the world which provides us with the things that are most stimulating, helpful, and energizing. When we are tired, our usual preference is to get into some kind of interaction with other people. It is a very common experience for persons who turn to the world first to come home from a long, tiring day and say: "Gosh, am I tired. Let's go next door and visit with the neighbors." The interaction, the staying involved in the world, for the most part, helps us. In fact, it energizes us.

There are other folks who tend to turn into themselves for the very strength that the first group finds by turning outside themselves. Carrying the marks of what Jung called introver-sion, these are the "me first" folks. When they are tired or troubled, private time and space provide the conditions most appropriate for recovery. While the "world first" folks tend to think out loud, the "me first" folks will think things through privately, and then will announce the results. The tongue-in-cheek way of describing them is to point out the times in which they have announced the solution to a problem that no one else knew existed! They don't always let other folks in on the processes that are important to them.

Bear in mind that all of us have "world first" and "me first" characteristics. But one of these orientations will be a greater preference for you than will the other. A helpful analogy is to think in terms of right-handedness or left-handedness. All other things being equal, we are able to use both hands. Most of us, though, have a preference as to which hand we will use more frequently and with greater comfort. The same is true with turning to the world or turning into the self. We are not consistent all the time, but our preferences do begin to come through as people come to know us and as we come to know ourselves. Now, what does this have to do with perception? There are unique perceptual strengths and liabilities to be found in each of these types.

The "world first" people are acutely aware of what is going on around them. In my own teaching of counseling, I find that these people are very conscious of body movement, facial expressions, changes in the environment, etc. They are quick to see and hear them, and they are quick to let us know about them. They are very much in touch with what's going on.

The second group, the "me first" folks, are very much in touch with what is going on inside themselves. They think more carefully and precisely, and they are able to carry out work without being as easily distracted because of changes or movements that are taking place around them. The preference for private space is very important for them to do their best work, and it is often difficult for them to understand the learning and problem-solving approaches of the other group.

Sometime ago I had the opportunity to work with a family whose teenage son had been running away from home with increasing frequency. Upon investigating what was going on, I found that the parents and two other siblings were all "world first" people. The son who was running away was very much a "me first" type. Consequently, whenever the son would return home, there would be immediate inquiries from other family members about "What's happening?" Sometimes, in desperation, the son would retreat to his room and close the door. Immediately, one or more family members would knock on the door and ask, "What's wrong?" Their need to be in touch was in conflict with his need to have private time and space. Eventually, he had learned that the only way to get private time and space was to leave and not let anyone know where he was going. That was an important difference that seemed to be a given within this family. Failure to accept that difference had resulted in great misunderstanding and some genuine conflict until they perceived what was really taking place. Those were roots, or givens, that the family needed to acknowledge. Perceiving the differences and acknowledging them gave that family new power to work for harmony and understanding.

What's Real/What's Possible

Under the terms of sensation and intuition, Jung identified further differences that exist among us. In fact, he called sensation and intuition specifically perceiving functions.

Sensation refers to our senses—seeing, hearing, tasting, smelling, and touching. Many of us want to know what is real, and we give primary attention to those things which are clearly provable. Thus, the "what's real" people tend to look for facts and details first. Concepts and ideas are less likely to catch their attention or interest. We "what's real" folks tend to be very good at working out the plan for getting something accomplished. One of my colleagues has described this as "working from the bottom up." We will build the structure step by step, and will tend to be skeptical about things that are not apparent to the senses.

No doubt, the disciple Thomas was a "what's real" person. In the Gospel of John, we are told that the other disciples told him, "We have seen the Lord." But he said to them, "Unless I *see* in his hands the print of the nails, and place my finger in the mark of the nails, and place my hand in his side, I will not believe" (John 20:25). Somewhat distrustful of dreams and illusions, the "what's real" folks are the ones who work out the fine print in the contract and the organizational method for keeping our world in motion.

On the other hand, there is a second group of very important people, whom I have chosen to call the "what's possible" crowd. These are the dreamers, the visionaries, the ones who are more fascinated with concepts and ideas than with facts and details. The dream of what may be possible is as real and believable to them as are the senses to our former group. Another colleague of mine tells the story of a married couple whom he saw in counseling. They had moved into a house prior to its being completed, and they found themselves in great conflict. The wife was a "what's real" person. Living in the house with sawdust, wood chips, constantly shifting furniture, and muddy floors was simply too much for her. She could see and hear all those disruptions, and it was driving her crazy. Her husband, who was a "what's possible" person, would come home every afternoon and look about the house with an excited, "This place is going to be great!" The very things that bothered his wife were literally not important to him. They were not the things that he perceived. Rather, he saw what it was going to be like in the future, and that was what mattered.

We "what's real" folks need the "what's possible" folks to keep us excited in our moments of discouragement. They need us to help work out the details to bring dreams true. Working in harmony, those two means of perceiving can bring great richness into our lives. But if those differences in perception are not understood, destructive conflict always hovers right around the corner.

Expectations

While more could be developed from Jung's studies about type and personality, I would like to turn to another way of understanding perception. We all carry within us expectations of what we want the world to be like, what we want ourselves to be like, and what we want other people in our lives to be like. Those expectations are clearer to some of us than to others. Whether we are clear about our expectations or not, they affect our moods, our responses to other people, and our general ability to function creatively. Conscious or not, we regularly "scan" to see whether our expectations are being met.

William Glasser, in his book *Stations of the Mind,* helps us understand the ways in which those expectations can affect the way we perceive and, more important, the way we act. He describes this process in terms of "comparing stations." Each of us has needs, hopes, and expectations. Our desire is to bring those things into being. Consequently, we look for opportunities to shape the world and our relationships according to our preferences. When we are unable to do so, frustration strikes, and some very important choices are made—choices that may help us to refine our expectations, find more effective means for working on the expectations, or make us give up, frustrating ourselves and others in the process.

Let me give an example. One of my needs and expectations is to be seen as a responsible and enjoyable person. Consequently, I have a regular "comparing station" that is open within myself and scans the world (remember that I am a "world first" person) for opportunities to be seen as responsible and enjoyable. Not long ago, my wife asked me if I would ride a "high-wheeler" bicycle in a living history exhibition put on by the museum for which she was working. I readily agreed. After all, I would be helping my wife, enjoying myself by trying something new, and I would be taking good care of the bicycle which was being loaned to the museum. The bike was quite expensive, and Kathy inquired several times as to whether I had made arrangements to transport it carefully, ride it safely, etc. Before long, I found myself getting irritated. My need to be seen as responsible was being interfered with by Kathy's frequent inquiries about whether I was taking good care of the bicycle. My need to enjoy myself was being interfered with by the fact that this was becoming quite a chore. The result was increasing irritation on my part, expressed toward Kathy. Unfortunately, my "comparing station" for being helpful to Kathy was blocked out by my other needs. Consequently, I missed spotting the anxiety under which she was laboring to bring a big program off successfully. My irritation and hostile behavior were reactions to my expectations' being frustrated, and my behavior was neither productive for me nor helpful to Kathy.

Fortunately, Kathy told me how my behavior was affecting her work. That confrontation helped me to discover and tell her what had been at stake for me. The discussion of our expectations helped us each, in Glasser's terms, to reopen our respective comparing stations concerned with helping each other. We each then became easier to work with because of our shared expectations.

Increased awareness of those expectations helped me. I recognized again how my expectations affect my perception. What I see first are those things which directly affect me. It takes some extra effort, and the help of other people, to help me perceive other things that deserve attention as well. That is simply a characteristic of being human. It is one of the roots of my existence and yours. Our expectations will always affect our perception, and we need to keep ourselves open to community and new education so that we will not confine ourselves in ways that are damaging and hurtful.

What Does It All Mean?

I want to refer you to our first chapter. Remember our discussions about finitude and distortion? The givens that we have been discussing in the present chapter are examples of the limits you and I possess and of the possible confusion that often takes place because of such perceptual characteristics.

Whether I am a "world first" or a "me first" person, I am limited by virtue of that preference. The same is true whether I am a "what's real" or a "what's possible" person. These givens, which are in me as a person, are examples of my imperfection. If I do not understand those limitations, or if I fail to perceive them, I will be very prone to skew things. The distortion can lead to an exaggerated or a diminished understanding of myself. Further, the ways in which I care for my neighbor and myself will be significantly bent out of shape. Indeed, my relationship with God will become confused.

Coming to terms with the givens of our nature is very important. One of the most important things to understand is that we cannot change them that drastically. It is more important that we understand them. The understanding itself will enable us to use these limitations as strengths, rather than make us feel ourselves caught up in a kind of slavery.

Take some time to look at yourself and the givens of your nature. You may think in terms of the examples in this chapter. You may want to expand your reflection to looking at your family history, your present relationships, and your involvements in the community. I am listing several books at the end of this book which you may find helpful if you would like to explore the subject in more depth. In the next chapter we will begin to look at some of the environmental influences that affect your perception.

Chapter 3

After the Givens

In the previous chapter, I placed a good deal of emphasis on the givens that come with us as individuals. That is not all there is to us, however. Remember the environmentalists of personality, who remind us of the conditioning that takes place as we grow and develop. Their emphasis on environmental influences in our growth process has come to be called developmental psychology.

The basic assumption of most writers and theorists in developmental psychology is that all of us move through a continuing series of stages. Each of these stages involves important tasks to be completed or learned. A successful putting together of these tasks contributes to our sense of health and well-being and prepares us for future developmental stages. An unsuccessful handling of these tasks results in less happiness and a fragile sense of well-being, as well as poor preparation for future stages of development.

Erik Erikson is the best known of the developmental writers. A painter of children's portraits in his earlier years, he came to be a noteworthy psychiatrist who specialized in working with children. Erikson describes the stages of development more extensively for the childhood years through adolescence. Other writers, such as Daniel J. Levinson, have expanded and revised Erikson's ideas about adult development.

Whom Do You Trust?

Erikson's earliest stage of development, and that of many other writers, revolves around the issue of trust. At birth and during infancy, we are absolutely dependent creatures. Nutrition, safety, and cleanliness all depend on the care and attention of others. Helpless as we may appear, a great deal of learning is taking place. One of the most important areas of learning has to do with trust and mistrust. Warmth from others, or the lack of it, teaches us much about responding to others.

We also develop some signals to watch for as infants. Just look at the procedure you use when meeting a new person. Have you ever gotten the sense that this person is not to be trusted, is even to be avoided? Or, on the other hand, have you not had times when you knew it was "love at first sight"? Or, if not love, at least you knew that this person was going to be a good friend.

Occasionally your intuitions are wrong, but for the most part you have developed a very elaborate system of detecting who is trustworthy and who is not. A large portion of that set of clues developed in infancy. You have refined them further as you matured in adulthood. These perceptions are based in large part on your early experiences. From time to time, you can even say that a person reminds you of someone from earlier years. And you will often decide about trusting the person on that basis. There are even occasions when you discover that such first impressions were wrong—that your perception had been contaminated by characteristics that reminded you of events from the past.

Voice tone, facial expression, physical stature, and choice of words—all are taken into account as your perceptual system weeds out those who are not trustworthy and seeks out those who are.

What Can I Do?

Another of the critical stages of development occurs during the elementary school years. Other stages of development occur in the interim, of course. This particular stage is another helpful example of environmental influences. It focuses on competence.

As you may remember, elementary school years are times of *doing* many things. Sports, science projects, social gatherings—all are oriented to the discovery of competence. And some very significant learning takes place about what you are able to do.

Your perception of your own competence is deeply rooted in the experiences of these elementary school years. For instance, some experiences during those times may have left you with questions about being able to finish anything. Such experiences may have come from very well intentioned motives on the part of a parent or a teacher. For instance, one of those significant persons could have seen you struggling with a project. Out of genuine desire to be helpful, the person may have moved in and said, "Here, let me finish that for you." Repeated enough times, that pattern can leave the notion that "I'm not able to finish things. After all, someone else always seemed to feel the need to come up and do it for me."

Another perception that might carry into adulthood from those years focuses more on the quality of our work than on our ability to finish. You may have finished many things.

Then a helpful adult would come in and say: "That's very good. Now, let me show you how to do it better." Again, well-intentioned. However, notice the long-term impact that it may have. You may then think your work is never quite good enough. Small wonder that in later years people have difficulty valuing what they do or perceiving themselves as competent.

Of course, positive experiences are possible as well. Left to struggle, given suggestions, or encouraged to try again, you may have developed a solid sense about your ability to follow through and experience satisfaction with your work. Consequently, when new work and new challenges appear, your perception is one that enables you to carry on rather than give up.

Who Am I?

We will discuss one other stage of development. Adolescence, as we all know, is a very crucial period in life. At that point, we move from "whom do we trust?" and "what can we do?" to careful scrutiny of ourselves. Certainly all these earlier stages do not disappear. We are still gaining information and learning about many others that we have not discussed. Still the real focus in adolescence is on self. After all, we are part of our environment, too.

The trust question, for instance, may now turn to ourselves. Are we trustworthy? What happens to us or to other people when we do not keep our promises, when we fall short of trust that is placed in us? Or, what are we worth if we do not see that our work is worth very much? If we have been left with a sense of never quite doing our work well enough, does that also mean that we are not quite measuring up?

All these questions and more begin to surge along with the

rapidly flowing hormones that come with the teenage years. "Faithfulness" becomes the watchword of this era. To whom and to what are we faithful? And who or what is faithful to us? Thus the questions about parents, friends, beliefs, vocation, etc., all surface with regularity and intensity.

Important decisions are made during these years. Often there is the decision of whether to marry. Commitments to religious beliefs are expected. Preparation for future work is encouraged. Success or failure in those decisions leaves you, again, with perceptions about your ability and your worth. And those perceptions are indeed powerful.

Family History

We have talked thus far about environmental influences as if they were quite individualistic. Note, however, that significant other people regularly appear as these stages move along. Of course, the most influential persons are in families. As the years move along, teachers become increasingly important. In adolescence, peers assume more and more significance. All of these later relationships, however, are affected by the particular family history or system from which you come.

A whole discipline of counseling and psychotherapy has evolved which is based on a model called family systems. I want you to have some information about this approach, because your family system also affects your perceptions.

One of the basic assumptions in the family systems approach to understanding yourself is this: If you are having difficulties, some relationship is involved. Think about that for a moment. If you have had a bad day, if your perception seems to be off, if you find yourself angry or saddened, probably something is happening in a relationship that is important to you. The relationship may be a historical one—that is, your difficulties may date to some of the developmental stages that we have been discussing. You did not receive the support or the trustworthy response that was so important to a sense of well-being. Because of that incompleteness in an important relationship early in your life, you are now feeling a great void.

Or, your bad day may be tied much more closely to a current relationship. Perhaps communication has not been going well with a spouse or a child or a supervisor. When that happens, the system in which you live preoccupies you and distorts your ability to cope with decisions and activities that are calling for your attention. If you have had an argument on the way out of the house in the morning, your perception is contaminated for a while because of that disrupted relationship. In other words, your environment has asserted its power over your ability to perceive and carry out tasks, even if they are unrelated to that unpleasantness of several hours or days ago.

You belong to many "families" in your daily existence. Certainly there is the immediate family of which you may be a part. There are work families, church families, club families, etc. Each of these has its effect on your perception, your ability to work, even your own sense of well-being. Those genetic factors discussed in the previous chapter will also affect your response to these environmental pressures that are exerted upon you.

Some families, when experiencing prolonged difficulty, seem to "produce" a person who is more visibly upset or upsetting than are the other members. It is as if the family has become a body and chosen one of its parts to be the symptom of the difficulty. When we see this kind of situation developing, we can understand more about the description of the church as a body and about the various members of the church being its parts. When the body is ill, the parts show the symptoms of the illness. That is the case with the families of which we are a part. And at times we may find ourselves serving as the symptom! When that happens, it is not just our perception that is affected negatively. We are simply reflecting the fact that *everyone's* perception is turning out to be negative.

A system is a cluster of relationships. Be it immediate family, close friends, or working partners, the cluster teaches "correct" ways to respond and conduct yourself. You are taught more than behavior by these clusters. You are also taught how to perceive. You are trained to "get with the system!"

But different systems have different perceptions. Take anger, for instance. In one environment, anger may be understood as a normal expression of emotion. In fact, to "get your anger out" is encouraged because it is perceived to be healthy. In another system, however, anger may be perceived as damaging, with resulting punishment for those who express it.

Your system of relationships has left you with many learned ways of perceiving things. Many prejudices exist and endure in you and me; so does strength of character. We owe much of the credit to those influential networks of relationships in which we have lived and are living.

Chapter 4

Belief
and Perception

We come with certain givens. We respond to a variety of influences as we continue to grow. A third crucial area that exerts power upon our perception is belief. Certainly the first two factors influence the kinds of beliefs we have. Our disposition may find more comfort in some beliefs than others. Our family and other environmental influences may push us more strongly toward some beliefs than others. But, in the final analysis, our beliefs are also a matter of choice. And what we believe deeply colors what we are able to perceive and thus the possibilities and limits that we see for ourselves.

To help us get a firmer grasp on the power of belief, let us look at some of the difficult and painful areas of our lives. We will talk about the effect that our belief has on the way we perceive suffering and how we respond to it.

One of the first images that came to mind as I began thinking about this issue was that of a man from many years ago, whom I did not know. I was a hospital chaplain visiting from room to room on my assigned floor. This man had returned to his room following a leg amputation the day before my visit. When I entered the room and introduced myself, he said: "I'm glad you're here. I want you to pray for my leg to grow back." His request came from a set of very clear beliefs. First, he believed in God. Second, he believed that God loved him. Third, he believed that faith could move mountains. In short, he believed in a providential God who would intervene in very concrete ways on behalf of those who had faith. Consequently, in the days and weeks that followed, he resisted attempts at physical therapy and conversations about an artificial limb. He only prayed. To engage in the other activities would be "unfaithful" to the God in whom he believed.

A second image came to me as well. It was an image that was portrayed in the words of a young and sensitive artist whose name was Charlotte. She wrote: "It is my nature as a human being to remind people of the suffering they would so gladly turn away from. But I have never forgotten to make it plain that I love life with all my heart. And to love life, you have to consider its dark side—death—you must include suffering in your thoughts and understand it. To all those whom I love, I wish hard experiences that will make them look within themselves. For to feel compassion for others, we must have borne our own cross." Those words were written not long before Charlotte was arrested by the Gestapo on the evening of September 21, 1943. She died in the gas chambers of Auschwitz at the age of twenty-five. Her belief enabled her to perceive life in a way that made even the experience of such a senseless death meaningful.

Belief. What do we believe, and how does it mold the way we respond to the circumstances of our lives? How can we make sense out of leg amputations and cancer and murders and starvation and energy problems and wars and rumors of wars? What can we believe that will help us with our perception? How powerful can our perception be in the face of such difficult moments?

At base, our beliefs are a search for an explanation. If we have some way to understand what is taking place, then we can see what to do. Thus we look for the beliefs that will enable us to understand who we are as human beings and what the circumstances are that influence us. With such an understanding, we can rise above some of the more difficult situations in life and find solutions that are more faithful and caring. Our capacity to believe is a gift from God. Let's look together at some of the ways in which that belief may manifest itself around the issue of suffering.

It Must Be God's Will

One of the first beliefs about suffering that clearly affect your perception is centered around the issue of *justice*. Concern about justice lies behind the belief that various illnesses and tragedies are God's will. You can see this particular belief showing itself in questions such as, "What is it that we have done to have God punish us in this way?" Note that in this belief God is given full credit for various events, both good and bad. And the further notion is that there is justice in what God has chosen to do. When the fairness of a certain situation is not visible, the explanation is often, "You are not yet strong enough in the faith to see," or "God has not chosen to make his purposes clear to you yet."

This kind of belief about suffering works very well for many people. It's an attitude that gets us out of having to question God. Even if the suffering may seem unjust, we still quickly affirm that God is in control. And that is the second need which is satisfied with this particular belief: God is in control. The sense of assurance that God is using, indeed causing, tragic events in our lives gives great courage and comfort to many people. And such interpretations can be made not only in personal tragedy but also in international affairs. Much of the appeal of this deep belief in God's justice is that everything is assumed to have a purpose. Consequently, when tragedies occur, we can be assured that God had some plan in mind. After tornadoes, floods, and earthquakes, some people point to the event as a sign that God is trying to tell us something. At a more private level, when personal moments of failure come, it is a normal event to begin to look for the cause. Somehow, if we can find the point of our responsibility, the event will make sense. If the event is somehow *non*sense, coping with it becomes much more difficult.

When, in your perception, there "ain't no justice" in the world, you become confused. When you have worked hard, and a tragedy occurs, it is scary, because God suddenly appears to be undependable or unfair or unjust. So you start looking for an explanation—quickly, so you don't lose faith in the God that you want!

Notice that this particular belief carries with it several results. When something goes wrong, we perceive that there is fault to be found somewhere. Our action tends to be one that searches out that cause. A second perception is that God has a very direct involvement in whatever has taken place. A great deal of responsibility is placed there as well. We will return to these observations after looking at a second belief that can affect our response to suffering.

The Devil Did It

A second kind of belief, to which many people turn in times of suffering, looks for another responsible party. One of the more complicated expressions of this attitude is that "the dysteleological surplus of human misery is an achievement of demonic malevolence." While I cannot remember where I first ran into this fancy phrase, maybe you can impress your friends with it! Loosely translated, it means, "The devil did it." More carefully phrased, it means that the world is in the grip of evil powers. Evil exists. And God has allowed it in the decision to allow freedom in the way creation works.

As you can see, this belief is an attempt to place responsibility for suffering somewhere else. In fact, this attitude is another kind of reply to the query, "How could a loving God do such a thing?" The answer is that God didn't do it. Some power other than God did, and that other power is the appropriate object for any anger or sense of injustice. The concern here, too, is for justice. But this belief takes the heat off of God.

Interestingly enough, there is great similarity in both of these beliefs. They have a common bond in their expression of the wish that things were other than they are. In the first case, God is bound to bring about suffering because we have fallen short of his expectations of us. In this second case, an evil power has brought about these things that are out of our control. In either case, God is on our side in his wish that we did not have to go through the suffering.

There is very real comfort that comes from this second belief. That is one of its primary advantages to many people. In the perception that God does not want this to happen, we can feel comforted and cared for. Perception of an evil power of some kind, even if it is just luck, gives us a place to focus our anger and sense of unfairness. There still is a strong attempt to understand what has taken place, and this belief again furnishes an explanation.

God Is with Us

A third belief about God's involvement with suffering centers primarily on his being present with us. One way of describing this belief is that we do not know the exact nature of God's involvement with us. It is both a mystery and a certainty. That is to say, we don't know enough about God to know *what* he does or *how* he does it, but we know that *he is here* with us in his doing of it. As my friend and colleague, Sibley Towner, puts it in some comments on Job, "It suggests a life-style based not upon fear of God's perfect justice and his determination to exact an eye for an eye, but rather upon awe and wonder at God's willingness to be *for* us, even on a dunghill" (*How God Deals with Evil,* p. 117). What we are really describing here is the knowing and comforting quality of God's work with us. We may at times be angry because we don't understand, but we are still assured of a consistent and predictable involvement that we can depend on rather than wonder about. For all that we do not know, we do know one thing—that God is with us.

This particular belief has several positive features. First, you are relieved of the problem of being presumptuous enough to think you can come up with or have to come up with an explanation on behalf of God. Both of the earlier beliefs require you to do a great deal of explaining to save yourself and other people from seeing God as either helpless or mean.

Second, this belief frees you to care for people who cry out in pain or joy, instead of forcing you to explain everything to them. Our tendency with both of the earlier beliefs is to respond to people with words of explanation (often to get ourselves off the hook!) rather than with hand extended.

Third, this belief relieves many of the contradictions that appear in an appeal to justice or evil as the evidence of God's activity. As you can begin to say you don't know how God operates, you don't have to be rushing about looking at past events in order to prove somehow that God is still around.

Fourth, this position does not force you to see God as being in the trapped position of disciplinarian. To the contrary, you see God standing by you, picking up and comforting you when you experience difficulties in life. In fact, this position actually acknowledges that God hurts with you, and frees you to respond in very different ways.

So what do you do when you sit with a family whose child has just died? Explain it? Who would have the audacity to do that? Tell them that God had a purpose in it? Not me. Hear them cry out their anguish and their outrage at their sense of unfairness? Yes. Certainly. And to their question of why this happened, you respond in honesty, "I don't know." But even in that response there is an affirmation of faith. It is a belief that somehow, even though you do not understand, you believe that God is present with you and them in this situation. You have the opportunity to be responsible and creative, and even to learn from the consequences.

The Power of Your Perceptions

We might have picked many other areas to use as an example of the power that belief has on our perception. However, suffering is probably the area in which the question arises most crucially. *What* you believe makes a profound difference in your perception of the world and the way you live out your life in it. If you are willing to be responsible and to discipline yourself and are looking for belief that is faithful to God's word, you have new power at your disposal.

I hope that during this discussion you have reflected on the beliefs you have during times of suffering. Do you find yourself desperately looking for an explanation? If so, that really strips you of some of the power you have at your disposal. What you see (perceive) during difficult moments is a threat to your understanding of the world; your energy can become consumed by trying to explain yourself out of it. That really strips you of much of the power that is available to you.

During difficult moments, do you tend to write off the whole thing as irresponsible, a result of luck, or some evidence of the power of evil in our world? If so, you may again deny some of the power that is available to you. It's difficult to do battle with fate and evil powers. Thus, there may be a tendency to give up and wait to see what will happen next. Again, such a belief results in a perception of the world that strips you of much of the possibility that may exist.

However, if you believe in a God who is present with you, who gives you power to transcend the situation and to look for new possibilities, then your perception is broadened and enriched. Perception is a valuable gift. Certainly some time may be needed to express frustration and to question. But that can be freely expressed rather than cautiously muttered. You are free to move beyond the event and look for new possibilities. Certainly you will temper the possibilities with a knowledge of your limitations. But at the same time you may identify new gifts. As those gifts are perceived, you can experience even more power with God's grace.

Part II

CHANGING
YOUR
PERCEPTIONS

Chapter 5

Developing Good Sense

A discussion of changing your perception first draws upon your good sense. Perception is a noun which refers to information that you take in and organize. Of course, you take things in through your senses—what you see, hear, smell, taste, and touch. Needless to say, it is impossible for you to take in everything that is going on around you. That is part of the meaning of finitude, which we discussed in an earlier chapter. While you may not realize it, you are a very selective creature about what you allow yourself to perceive or take in through your senses.

That limitation on what you take in is the very cause of many of your difficulties in living. It is almost as if you decide not to perceive something that is unattractive or disturbing. You may be limited, but you are also very powerful in your ability to screen out undesirable information.

This chapter, then, will focus on important things that you need to understand and do to broaden your horizons. In other words, you have to work very hard to save yourself from the temptation to ignore things that you don't want to know or that you simply have not considered as a possibility. Why do we do such screening? It saves us from pain in the short run. However, our body's automatic responses to save us from pain in the short run can often lead to greater difficulties in the long run. We have to go into training to save ourselves from ourselves on such matters. So, let's begin to move through some of our senses in our quest to develop and use *good* sense.

Seeing Is Believing

You've heard that old phrase many times: "Seeing is believing." It really is true. The problem, however, is that it fails to acknowledge how much you *choose* what to see.

We need to talk about seeing in two ways. The first is in terms of actual movements or pictures that we take in. The second is in terms of the interpretations that we may make of those pictures. For instance, on a rainy day, my neighbor and I will both look out and see rain coming down. My immediate interpretation, if the grass is high, is: "What a relief! Now I can't mow the grass." My neighbor's reaction is: "What a disappointment! I was really looking forward to working in the yard today." We have both seen the same thing. Yet we have seen two very different things. Much of what we each have seen is controlled very much by our respective internal needs, desires, and sources of enjoyment.

Another example of differences in perception can be illustrated by two roommates who are working with a dresser drawer that is stuck. The first person sees that the drawer won't move. He or she tugged at it, found it uncooperative, saw that it was jammed, then sat back on the bed and said: "I can't open the drawer. See, it's stuck." The other roommate looks at the drawer, sees that the drawer is out of line, and says: "Oh, it's no problem. See, it's only pushed in crooked." He or she then straightens the drawer, opens it, and all is well. Again, both of them saw the same thing, yet they saw very different things.

Incidents such as those described above can be amusing primarily because they are not of great significance. However, our perception in terms of what we see continues under far more serious circumstances. Take two different married couples, for instance. With one couple, an intense discussion begins. The husband, as the conversation grows more intense, begins to look at the floor instead of into his wife's eyes.

"See what you're doing," accuses the wife. "You're not listening to me. You're just looking at the floor." The husband does not reply to her statement. The conversation becomes more bitter, and the wife feels more and more ignored because of what she has "seen."

In a second couple, the same initial maneuvers take place. However, when the wife accuses the husband of not listening, he replies: "I'm looking at the floor so I can concentrate on what you're saying. If I watch you, I get distracted." The wife, appreciative of that clarification, continues with her remarks. Eventually, the couple work their way through the difficulty.

Behavior on the part of both husbands was the same. In the case of the first couple, communication became worse because perception was not checked out. The second couple was able to move on more successfully with the conversation because the wife was able to change what she saw, at least the interpretation or perception of what she saw. Remember, though, that the change was made with the husband's help.

That is the critical piece about seeing. All of us have a tendency to see things from a particular perspective. When a child is angry, we may see rebellion rather than frustration or fatigue. When a spouse looks irritable, we may see him or her to be angry with us and may not investigate the source of the irritation. When a committee seems confused or uncooperative, we may presume that it is reacting to something we have done. Our perception is making an interpretation of the visible activity going on around us.

William Glasser provides us with some helpful understanding about all of this. In his book *Stations of the Mind,* he points out that our perception is very much controlled by the way we want things to be. For instance, the wife in our example wanted her husband to listen to her. She then searched for evidence that he was doing so. Further, she had certain criteria that would serve as proof that he was listening. When his behavior did not fit with her planned perception, she became angry, assuming that she *knew* that he was not listening. Her behavior was an attempt to get him to listen in the way she wanted to be listened to. In terms of power, note the strength that perception has on the way we respond to each other. Upon seeing something in a particular way, all sorts of spin-offs can occur. Perception has the power to set off a series of events for good or for ill. Just as the cowboys in the old Western movies saw danger when some Indians would ride to the top of the hill, so we may have been trained to see things in a particular way. Only later in my growing up could I understand that Indians were not always an enemy. There was another way of "seeing" them.

Consequently, one of the important things you can do about your own perception is learn to see more. It's important that you get reports from others about what you see. You need eyes other than your own. The very power that is exerted by what you see calls you to become more responsible about your actions. The very power that you have should encourage you to "check things out" with someone you respect.

What I Hear You Saying Is . . .

Just as vision has great impact upon our perception, so does hearing. A mother, father, and an eleven-year-old child were sitting in a family therapist's office. The mother began the conversation by saying: "I'm angry at our child lately because she keeps saying she's bored. It's not my responsibility to entertain her. She's old enough to think of things to do by herself. How dare she say to me she's bored?"

The husband responded: "That's interesting. I don't get angry when she says that. I understand it to be a request for suggestions of things to do. If I have something to suggest, I will say so. If not, I agree that she needs to be more creative herself. However, I don't think she is demanding that I program her day. She's only inviting me to give suggestions if I happen to have any."

Bemused, the child then said: "Neither one of you knows what I mean. I was just making a comment as I walked through the room. Am I never supposed to let you know how I'm feeling?"

Look at all the different reactions that come from one very simple set of words. Certainly, the things that we can see affect our interpretations of the words. But particular sets of words themselves can set off reactions in us without any other cues. I can still remember with delight the first time I read Virginia Satir's book *Conjoint Family Therapy*. In that book, she illustrates a variety of different interpretations that can be made of one very simple sentence: The dog is on the couch. Between her suggestions about the meanings of that sentence and my own additional interpretations, there were almost twenty different possibilities for what those words could mean. And the possible ways of hearing it could result in responses that ranged from amusement to anger to guilt to merely passing the time of day.

We are influenced heavily by our history and the meanings that certain words have had for us in our past. We also are limited by advance plans that we may make for a particular relationship. Those expectations can set our perception in motion long before any words are spoken to us. The problem is complicated further by the fact that most of us are very poor communicators. We are not very precise with our words, and that leaves much room for other people to hear what we say in vastly different ways.

One of the most helpful books I have seen in recent years is *The Structure of Magic*. The authors, John Grinder and Richard Bandler, point out that the therapists who seem to be the most effective in working with people for change are those who pay careful attention to the grammar their clients use. In other words, counselees are pushed to be specific when they speak. If their sentence structure has no predicates, if antecedents of pronouns are not clear, or if prepositions have no objects, the therapist pushes the client to complete the sentence structure. The results are often amazing. The sentence structure itself reveals the lack of clarity in the person's thinking. Being pressed to make clear and complete sentences, people begin to reveal what the authors call their "deep structure." The words being said first reveal the incomplete thinking and perception that is taking place. When clients are pushed to speak more precisely and listen to themselves, change of a positive nature begins to take place within them.

Who would have thought it! All that our English teachers tried to beat into our heads has inestimable value—and power! The power of words, and thus the impact of the way you listen to others and to yourself, is quite awesome.

Out of respect for the power of your sense of hearing, it is important to be very careful about the words you use and about the interpretations you make of your own words and the words of others.

Think of the New Testament writer James in his discussion of the power of the tongue. "If we put bits into the mouths of horses that they may obey us, we guide their whole bodies. Look at the ships also; though they are so great and are driven by strong winds, they are guided by a very small rudder wherever the will of the pilot directs. So the tongue is a little member and boasts of great things. How great a forest is set ablaze by a small fire!" (James 3:3–5).

The blazes that you set afire with your words or by your hearing of other persons' words can indeed do great damage. It is important that you train yourself more effectively in listening and in speaking, because of the power that the perception of the meanings of words can carry.

Getting Our Feelings Out

Along with vision and hearing, one of the popular measures used in decision-making in our day is "feelings." The decade of the 1960s and its strong emphasis on sensitivity and encounter have exaggerated the importance and thus the power of feelings. Many phrases, such as "getting our feelings out," "going with the flow," and "getting in touch with the self," sensitized us to the importance of emotion. Unfortunately, many expressions of that movement tended to encourage us to pay attention *only* to feelings. Bandler and Grinder speak of feelings as well. It is one of the "representational systems" on which we rely for our perceptions. The representation is kinesthetic, which means a response to touch or body sensation.

The condition of our bodies, including our emotions, certainly changes our perceptions of things and people. A common illustration of this comes with the observation of a child who is whining. Often, we know that the whining is a result of fatigue; the child has not had a nap, has been playing hard, has been ill, etc. Whatever the cause, the fact that the body is functioning at less than its normal state explains the abnormal behavior.

As an adult, you know that fatigue influences your perception and thus your ability to receive information, respond appropriately to other people, or do a job well. Stress has become a popular word in our day. It refers to the state of weariness in which we often find ourselves when we are overextended. Results of stress include inability to take in new information, repeatedly using one solution to a problem even though it doesn't work, irritability, increased blood pressure, listlessness, and insomnia.

If you are fatigued and irritable, even the welcoming cry of a child on your return home may become a cause for irritation. The excitement can be perceived as a request for time and attention, becoming one more interference with work or need for sleep. Consequently, because of the power that your emotions and bodily state carry, it is important for you to give close attention to taking care of your body. According to Scripture, you should think of your body as being a temple. You must respect, care for, and recognize the power that it holds.

Using Common Sense

Three of the senses that help form our perception have been discussed. Certainly we could talk much more about smells, taste, and the importance of touch and the other bodily sensations. I suggest that you let your own imagination explore these.

Your position is deeply shaped by your senses. The behavior in which you engage as a result of what you perceive is crucial. Thus it is very important for you to structure a program of preventive maintenance in the interest of respecting and caring for the power of your perception.

How can you go about this? It really is a matter of common sense. Rely on *all* your senses, rather than on one alone. Recognize that you are part of a larger community. The perceptions that you share with your family and friends will result in actions that are far more responsible and appropriate. Commonality is a matter of community. Our common sense calls for discovering the things that we can agree upon in mutuality. It does not mean that we must always agree with the group, but it does mean that we should check out our perceptions with others.

For instance, when I come home at the end of the day and hear my child crying upstairs, it would probably be better for me to ask my wife what has happened and to ask my daughter what has happened before I proceed to send her to her room for creating so much commotion. Good common sense tells me that I cannot know what has taken place before I came through the door. Therefore, I should not react as if I did know. Yet that is the temptation which many of us have.

Think back to the assumptions we discussed in the first part of this book. I am a limited creature. Thus, I cannot know what has taken place before I come through the door, since I am not all-knowing. At the same time, there may well be some gifts that I could bring to this particular situation since I was not there earlier. To inquire first about the perceptions of others will enable me to use my perception in a careful and responsible way. Then, I may be able to relieve my wife, who is tired; provide some comfort to my daughter; and in the long run, have a more peaceful evening myself. At the same time, my human limitations need to be remembered, lest I assume that I am the only one who can take care of the difficulty. After some careful inquiry, my perception may tell me that it is better for me to stay out of whatever is taking place between my daughter and my wife, so that they can work out their difficulties themselves without having an intruder trying to "shape them up."

Careful work needs to be done on checking out what you see, making sure you have understood what you have heard, and keeping your body in good shape so that your best abilities are available. In the next chapters, we will begin to look at some particular forms of stress and difficulty.

Chapter 6

Moving Past Depression

Depression is one of the experiences in life about which people are becoming more and more aware. Statistics vary on its definition and frequency, but a generally acceptable description is that at least 12 percent of the adult population has had or will have an episode of depression that is serious enough to require some sort of professional treatment. Further, during any given year, 15 percent of adults will suffer some sort of depression that hinders their interaction with friends, family, and work.

While enormous strides have been made in chemical treatment for depression, there seems to be more and more agreement that depression is tied very closely to perception, and successful treatment will also take it into account. We will use this chapter to examine depression and the power at your disposal for coping with it and for not allowing yourself to be captured by it.

In the Beginning

Let's move far beyond modern medical descriptions of depression to gain an understanding. One of our most helpful resources is the Bible. Certain biblical stories teach us a great deal about depression.

First, recall Saul, the king of Israel. The story is recorded in I Samuel 9–31. Chosen by God to be king, he went into battle with the Amalekites. His orders from God were to destroy everything. Instead, he allowed himself to be persuaded by his soldiers that the spoils should be divided among them. Samuel let Saul know of the Lord's displeasure with him for disobeying instructions, and God's favor upon him was ended.

From that point on, the Bible describes Saul as a tormented man. He is overcome with a sense of guilt, frequently expresses anger, and longs for consolation. David comes into the story at this point as a player of the harp and consoles Saul with his music. Saul continues to display the movement of mood back and forth, angry at times, despairing at others. David becomes more and more popular, and eventually his popularity is seen by Saul as further evidence that David is now the recipient of God's favor.

Saul moves for consultation with the Witch of Endor, who prophesies that he is doomed to die. A battle follows soon after. Perceiving his army to be losing, Saul orders one of his soldiers to kill him. When the soldier refuses, Saul falls on his own sword and kills himself.

A second story that is helpful to us is that of Cain and Abel, recorded in Gen. 4:1–16. Many of us have assumed that Cain killed Abel in a fit of anger, but if you read that story carefully you find that Cain's face falls when he discovers that his offering to the Lord has been refused. Abel's offering, on the other hand, was accepted.

The *sense of the fallen face* is, certainly in the Eastern mind, an expression of shame, lamentation, disappointment, or despair. That description of anger and despair, accompanied by disappointment, characterizes what we would now call depression. It leads, as you well know, to Cain's killing Abel in an outburst of rage as he is trying somehow to deal with the despair into which he has fallen.

One final illustration is the story of Job. Stripped of his belongings, his children, and his hopes, Job endures a long period of questioning, self-isolation, and resentment of his friends who come to give him advice. The outbursts of anger, the despondency, and the despair are all typical of what we would now describe as depression.

Note that there are some commonly shared characteristics in the three stories. The first is that of *expectation*. There are needs, desires, perceptions of the way the world ought to be. Saul wants to be king and in God's favor. Cain wants his gift valued and perceives himself deserving of his brother's birthright. Job, having served well, is confused that his desires have not been met when he has certainly followed the "formula." Whenever we look at depression, we can be sure that some expectation lies deep within the person about the way things ought to be.

Second, and clearly implied already, is the realization that the *expectation is not met*. The Lord does not look with favor upon Saul for disobeying his commands. Cain's offering is not looked at with favor by God. Job's prosperity does not continue. The major expectation which has been a moving force in a person's life does not come through.

That leads us to the third component, a *response*. The response that we are really discussing here is that of depression. Depression, for instance, may be a desperate attempt to make the expectation legitimate. At the very least, the experience of depression *might* bring in a system of support and agreement that the person deserved to have his or her expectations met. While the depression may not have been planned consciously, it certainly serves a function, or it is an attempt to serve a function. One of the responses to Saul's depression was a great deal of indulgence on the part of those who surrounded him. Unfortunately, he did not get the kind of indulgence from God that he desired. Cain desired his father's blessing. His earlier sulking and unhappiness invited, even begged for, a kind of sympathy. Unfortunately, he did not get the kind of sympathy he desired. The same can be said of Job in his desire for an explanation for what had happened to him.

Depression, then, has been with us for a long time. The perception of unfulfilled expectations is clearly a large part of its makeup. The biblical examples that we have cited, and others, help us to see the shortsightedness of perceptions in the lives of Saul, Cain, and even Job. Each of these stories offers to us a wider range of perception so that we can more clearly understand our own lives and God's expectations of us.

And So It Continues

Modern understanding of depression finds new language and more careful description of the stories found in the Bible. Not only does that research frequently confirm the stories described earlier in this chapter but it also helps us to see more clearly our theological understanding of what it means to be human.

For instance, one of the major writers in the field of depression is Aaron Beck. In his helpful book, *Cognitive Therapy of Depression,* Beck talks about a "cognitive triad" which describes three major patterns to be found in a depressed patient.

The first pattern focuses on the negative view of self which the person holds. "He sees himself as defective, inadequate, diseased, or deprived" (p. 11). In a very real sense, we might say that this component describes an exaggerated sense of helplessness. The person becomes so highly conscious of limitations that it is difficult to see anything else.

Beck's second pattern describes the tendency of a person to interpret ongoing experience in a negative way. The world is seen as making unfair demands or presenting immovable obstructions to the pilgrimage in which the person is engaged. These obstructions are often seen as far more awesome than is really the case. As a professor in a seminary, I frequently must talk with students who have failed an important test, particularly one that is required for ordination. A frequent comment upon meeting is, "My life is ruined!" The assumption in that statement is that because of failure on a particular test, the rest of the person's future has been set. Usually the person is able to see, upon reflection, that this is not really the case. A depressive personality, however, would maintain that view and find it difficult to hear or see things differently.

Note again a genuinely religious connection. The issue is finitude. In this case, the human limitation is a narrow perception. The person is able to look at only a particular slice of time. And on the basis of one event that has just happened or is happening, the person then assumes that his or her whole world has come to a halt. The perception is indeed limited.

Such a limited angle of vision leads naturally into Beck's third pattern of a depressive syndrome: a negative view of the future. To tie this in with our spiritual concerns, it really means that a person is unable or unwilling to hope. The limited perception which we have talked about earlier results in a restrictive view of the future. Consequently, the person expects more of the same rather than the possibility of change.

Writers such as Beck have enabled us to analyze more critically the features that are going on in a person's thinking when he or she is affected by depression. William Glasser presses this even further by talking about depression as a kind of *choice*. In a sense, you *choose* to be depressed! The choice reinforces the limited perception which you already had. That limited perception is further reinforced by the reactions of other people, as well as in the depressed person himself or herself.

Glasser's observations are that depression, first, "allows us to perceive ourselves as helpless, because mostly we are" (*Stations of the Mind,* p. 160). The helplessness revolves around unfulfilled expectations. In a particular case we were unable to bring about those expectations, therefore we view ourselves as helpless in general. The depression reinforces our own sense of helplessness.

The second feature, which Glasser then notes, is that depression serves to keep our anger in check. The story of Cain and Abel reveals what can happen if anger is *not* kept in check. One temptation when our expectations do not come true is to get even with whatever has interfered with those wishes. That kind of behavior could get us into big trouble, so we find some other kind of behavior to keep us under control. Unfortunately, depression is far too extreme a method of keeping ourselves under control. It renders us even more helpless than we were before.

Third, being depressed, or depressing ourselves, is an indirect, hard-to-understand means of asking for help. Often, when we do not have the courage to admit our helplessness, appearing depressed results in getting the same response as if we had actually asked for help. But since we did not actually ask, a sense of pride can be maintained! A strange and circular logic it is, but some folks use it.

And fourth, Glasser notes that depression sometimes functions as a way of controlling other people. In feeling sorry for you, other people will meet your expectations in a way they would not have done had they viewed you as being more healthy.

Again, see the narrowness that is part of the depression. We might even discuss it as a kind of idolatry. Depression, in some of its manifestations, is a preoccupation with one particular expectation that we had set for ourselves. Having failed to obtain that expectation, nothing else matters anymore. Thus, we engage in strange forms of behavior, such as those described by Beck and Glasser.

So What?

These very brief references to some of the major work that has been done on what you can do about depression help in several ways. First, they help you to see that depression is a complicated matter. On the other hand, they reveal some very basic and essential characteristics of you and me as human beings. The major thing that they reveal is how the narrowness of our perception can affect us profoundly and painfully. You should also be alerted, however, to the ways that increased perception can save you and other people from the damage that depression brings. It is one of those strange things involved in the tension between freedom and determinism.

The freedom that you have to see yourself as a limited creature is, in its own way, a blessing. When I look at myself as limited, ironically, I become less limited. Simply because I know my shortcomings and my limits, I become more able to choose carefully and wisely the things that I undertake. When I fail at a major task, a limited view of myself may tempt me to get depressed. In that depression, I may feel sorry for myself, get others to feel sorry for me, and even excuse myself for my failure. After all, if I'm depressed, I can't be held responsible for my actions! In fact, I might even have been depressed when I took the test, and that would explain what happened. Regardless of all these rationalizations about being depressed, however, it does me no good in pursuing or revamping my expectation. I am not likely to take the test again, much less pass it, if I maintain my depression.

On the other hand, after failing a test, if I look carefully to see what areas I neglected to study, then I have allowed myself to see more than I had seen before. Recognizing the limitations enables me to become more focused as I prepare to take the test again. Another alternative, of course, is to discover that the test was in an area that was not that important or essential to my being. The failure becomes a point of transition, freeing me to shift my sights to other directions. That, too, is a recognition of limitations. This sort of recognition of limits, however, can energize me and enable me to move along rather than to settle into a depression of some kind and remain just as I was.

The effective counselor today has the courage to push people gently to look critically at the events going on in their lives. Such careful examination may enable them to see or perceive something that did not appear to them before. With that new perception, the need for depression diminishes, and the ability to learn increases.

Even our biblical stories become more insightful for us at that point. Saul, with increased perception, might well have been able to ask forgiveness and seek to reestablish his relationship with God. His depression, however, led him to withdraw into himself, showing little regard or willingness for maintaining any relationship with others, including God. Cain, too, suffered from the decreased appreciation for what was possible with God. Only Job, out of the three examples, stands as a model for coming to wider perception. In the midst of his self-indulgence and angry questioning of God, God's question to Job is, in effect, "Who are you to question anything that I have done?" The lesson is in many ways a reminder of our limitations and a call for obedience. God's grace itself is a reminder to us of our limits, an invitation to a greater vision of God and of ourselves, and thus a healing agent when our temptation is to remain depressed and withdrawn.

A Word of Caution

It is very important to remember that we have been talking about particular kinds of depression. There is increasing awareness of depression that is biochemical in nature. The technical term for this is endogenous depression. It arises from *within* the body. Such depressions are indeed well served by treatment with medication. Nonetheless, even with treatment by medication, a narrowing of perception comes about. A counseling process often enables a person to benefit more fully from the miraculous healing that medication brings.

It is also very important to recognize that none of us is totally aware of all the decisions that we make in response to a perception that we hold. It might be easy for you to conclude from my discussion that we should simply tell people who are depressed to "shape up or ship out." Nothing could be further from the truth. Depression is often subtle and sneaky. One of its most troublesome traits is the ability to convince you that you are far more helpless than you actually are. There may be times when it is important for us to push a person hard to broaden his or her perception. In other cases, gentleness—a persistent gentleness—may well be the most helpful aid that we can bring.

Depression has been used as an example here because of the frequency with which it occurs and because it illustrates so well the power of our perception. Depression may also be a by-product of grief. You may have lost someone or something very important to you. Your hopes or expectations have not come true. And so you retreat into yourself. To think of depression as being cured by perception is *one* of several helpful frames of reference for us to use.

To perceive implies that you are looking about, searching for information that will be helpful. When you have withdrawn into your grief, it is eventually important to look outside yourself for solace and consolation. The writers of the psalms teach us to describe our inner experience as well as to reach out to others who may comfort us. Their descriptions are poignant, such as the familiar words of Psalm 22: "My God, my God, why hast thou forsaken me? Why art thou so far from helping me, and from the words of my roaring? O my God, I cry in the daytime, but thou hearest not; and in the night season, and am not silent."

Words such as these describe grief, but they may also describe the pain of depression. Only as you recognize and claim the gift of community can you begin to move past your depression. Only as you recognize the importance of community can you see your responsibility to reach out to persons who are depressed and invite them to come along with you.

Both the psalmists and the psychiatrists teach us that recognition of our human condition is essential for growth. And further, they both remind us that forgiveness is an essential component in the process. Forgiveness says that I'm not going to hang on to that grudge anymore. Depression in many ways becomes a kind of grudge—an unwillingness to let go of the thing that preoccupies you. You hang on to it and don't want to let go. Forgiveness does not mean forgetting about the expectation that was so important to you. The memory will be important, but forgiveness does mean that you begin to let go of that expectation and look for others that are available to you. When you look, though, you also acknowledge that what you find won't be the same.

One of the most powerful examples of that inability to let go came to me in a phone call many years ago. When you're a minister, and your last name starts with *A*, you get some strange phone calls. In this particular case, a woman called with an important question: At the time of the final coming, would God judge those who had already died before those who were currently living, or would he judge those who were currently living before he judged those who had already died?

I confess to you that I did not have an answer at my fingertips! I resorted to another technique that could prove helpful to her (and give me some time!). I asked why she was asking the question. I'm glad I responded that way, because she then began to describe her son, who had become involved with another woman. That woman had borne his child. He had been unwilling to marry her, had gone to Vietnam, and there had been killed. This mother was afraid that if she did not have a chance to intervene with God on her son's behalf, he would be punished eternally.

Now that woman was very depressed. First, she was unable or unwilling to forgive her son for what he had done. At the same time, she was afraid and despairing of what might happen to him. For ten years, she had not been able to let go of that experience in her life. It had preoccupied and dominated all that she had done through that period of time.

In a real sense, I encouraged her to recognize the limits of what she could do for her son and to come to terms with her own inability to forgive him for so long. Only in the context of community, talking with a minister, could she begin to recognize what was taking place within her. Her perception increased, and in our several conversations she began to see that she needed to give up that preoccupying force in her life. Her admission of her limits meant that she had to rely on God instead of on herself. That kind of recognition, confession, sense of community, and forgiveness involved a widening of her perception. And what power was available to that woman after such recognition! She could genuinely live her life in a way that was concerned with the needs of others, rather than remain withdrawn and focused on her son. She could begin to grow again and look for other sources of meaning in her life. And she certainly could be a help to others.

Depression, as I have said earlier, is one example of an experience in life that calls for widened and enlightened perception. In the next chapter, we will look at stress, a more general human experience, but one that involves the power of your perception to a great extent.

Chapter 7

Perception and Stress

Depression, which we discussed in the last chapter, is a very particular form of stress. We discussed it first because of its common but not universal occurrence in our day. However, everyone suffers stress of one kind or another. This chapter will attempt to focus on the power that perception makes available to you in coping with many different forms of stress that come about in your life.

What Is Stress?

Many definitions are helpful to us in trying to understand stress. Hans Selye, one of the foremost authorities on the topic, provides a very simple definition: Stress is the nonspecific response of the body to any demand (*The Stress of Life*, rev. ed., pp. 34–36). In other words, when something is demanded of you, and there is not immediate clarity on how to respond, your body begins to try out a number of responses all at the same time. The nonfocused nature of those responses is what we would call stress.

Another way of talking about stress is in terms of a simple dictionary definition. One such illustration is "any interference which disturbs the organism at any level and produces a situation which is natural for the organism to avoid." Note that this particular definition emphasizes disturbance and the need to flee. Many pressures that you experience trigger that very kind of response.

In a helpful article in *Time* magazine (June 6, 1983), the authors note the price of civilization. At the dawn of human history, when something threatening appeared, there was a simple choice to be made: fight or run. However, in more civilized society, when traffic is racing at us on the streets, when bosses are demanding more results, when customers are furious, when requests continue to be made for our time—the choice to fight or run is not really an option for us. Hence, the zooming sales of Maalox, Tagamet, and other anxiety relievers. We avoid by trying to do away with the *symptoms* of stress.

A psychologist friend of mine, Dr. Ed. Hampe, speaks of stress as a ratio of demands to resources. When you have the resources available to meet the demands that are placed upon you, you have a healthy level of stress. If the demands exceed the resources that you have, the stress becomes negative. If your resources far exceed the demand, there is another kind of stress—boredom. Hampe helps us to understand that stress is not always a negative thing. It is simply a part of our humanness, and our aim is to understand stress and handle it better through the power of our perception.

The Effects of Stress

So we know how to describe stress. It may be nonspecific. It may be a need to run or fight. It may be something we can talk about in very sophisticated fashion as a mathematical formula. The main thing, however, is what it does to you.

One of the first things that happens to you under stress is

that your perception level diminishes. As your body is gearing itself up to respond to something out there, it becomes so focused on finding the enemy that it is not inclined to look for ways to understand what is happening or what to do about it. A simple example is an animal that is caught by headlights and is focused on the enemy but frozen in terms of response. We can become just as immobilized if stress is high.

It is interesting to see that on the personality inventory discussed earlier in this book, the Myers-Briggs Type Indicator, "perceiving" people tend to be those who enjoy processing data more than they enjoy making decisions. They continue to broaden their perception, but the result is often a slowness about deciding anything. On the other hand, "judging" people tend to push hard to get a decision made and may well neglect getting adequate information.

When we are under stress, our temptation is to focus on one interpretation or continue collecting the same data over and over again. A simple example of decreased perception level occurs regularly in my office. I am so convinced that a missing paper is right there on the desk that I continue to search the desk top over and over again. It never occurs to me to look on top of the filing cabinet next to the desk, which often is the very place where the paper I have lost is located.

Watching people learn how to sail can provide another example. It is very difficult for them to perceive that direction can be changed by adjusting the sails as well as by moving the rudder. In fact, to concentrate on one of those options to the exclusion of the other can result in some pretty uncomfortable and even dangerous situations.

All of this is to say that stress has the effect of closing down your perception system. You may even regress to old patterns of behavior, no longer having more successful patterns even available to you in your memory. You will be prone to lock in to responses whether or not they work. In the most extreme instance, fatigue and depression may occur, or even physical and emotional illness.

Stress in Relationships

The area of living that is most gratifying and stressful is that of relationships. Look at the soaring rate of divorce. Think of the headaches, flushed faces, and stomach twists that occur when a relationship is not going well. Think also of the sense of exhilaration and even dizziness that can take place when something special has happened in a relationship. Positive events are stressful for you just as negative ones. Inventories designed to measure stress demonstrate this in their listings: marriage, divorce, job loss, promotion, etc.

In relationships, it is not at all unusual for us to see the perception level decrease when some kind of stress takes place. One of the most helpful illustrations of how that can take place is provided by Virginia Satir in her book *Peoplemaking*. Satir has pointed out on earlier occasions that successful communication demands that we give attention to at least three dimensions. The first is self. It is very important for us to understand ourselves, including our needs, our desires, our history, our temptations, etc.

The second dimension that calls for attention is the other person. It is equally important to work hard to understand that other person's needs, desires, hopes, history, and temptations.

Further, as a third dimension, it is important to understand the context of the particular relationship. What are the agreements that have been made about the nature of our association? If we are married, there are expectations about faithfulness. If we are close friends, particular agreements about confidentiality may be important. Of course, the assumptions made about marriage or friendship may differ very much between the two individuals who are involved. Hence the importance of working hard to understand the self and the other person. Such understanding results in better understanding and agreement about the nature of the relationship.

Note that maintenance of a good relationship, then, demands that you have a broad perceptual field. You need to be tending to self, other persons, and context on a regular basis. What Satir notes so helpfully in her book is the narrowing of perception when there are difficulties. For instance, you may, when under stress, begin to ignore yourself. Becoming so focused on helping the other person, you may pay attention only to him or her, neglecting your own needs. The later result may be resentment and even sabotage of the relationship because of his or her perceived neglect. Perceiving your own contribution to the neglect of self comes hard.

Other stress responses are possible, however. Under stress you may choose to ignore everyone else in favor of yourself. Or, you may ignore both your own needs and those of others in order to reduce life to a set of rules. Such behavior, in exaggerated fashion, focuses on the context of the relationship.

Stress can engender any of these narrowed perceptions. But I trust that you will quickly note the dangerous effects that can come from such a reduction in perception. When I begin to make decisions strictly on the basis of *my* needs, then the relationship is subject to damage. In fact, even I am subject to greater damage. As I focus on myself, my temptation will also be to forget about my finitude and my temptations. Thus my choices will be far from wise. An interesting illustration of what can happen is provided by a mother and a daughter whom I know. The mother had left a set of instructions about responsibilities for the daughter to undertake. Upon returning home, she assumed that the daughter would not have done any of the tasks, and walked into the kitchen with the question, "Well, why didn't you clean up the kitchen?" The daughter immediately replied: "You didn't even look to see if I had. You just thought you knew. That's all you ever do—accuse first and ask later."

Relationships provide all sorts of opportunities for stress. That stress comes about because of our failures in communication. Our perception is often limited, and we need to work hard at broadening it so that we can give attention to many dimensions at one time instead of limiting ourselves to one.

Stress and Anger

When you are threatened and under stress, one of the temptations you may have is to become angry. Anger is not always a matter of choice, but the way in which we deal with it certainly is.

The Bible is full of statements that indicate that anger in and of itself is not bad. Ephesians 4:26 tells us, "Be angry, but do not sin; do not let the sun go down on your anger." The indication there is that anger itself is not evil. But some very specific suggestions are given about the proper handling of anger in order to avoid a sinful expression of it.

The observation in this verse, which is certainly clarified in much psychological study, is that anger, too, tends to diminish our perception. We become preoccupied with the rightness of our position, or the wrongness of the other person's view. Then it is difficult for us to understand anything beyond that distinction.

Much work has been done in conflict resolution to help us

gain more power by expanding our perception. Therefore, a typical method for resolving conflict often includes an agreement that the persons postpone working on the problem until the anger has had some time to diminish. The danger of such a postponement is that the issue will not be dealt with at all. Therefore, the formulas are very precise about the importance of setting a time to deal with the issue.

Taking advantage of the elapsed time, two parties can then sit down and, in a very disciplined manner, give each person time to talk about his or her perception of what has happened. A critical part of this conversation is that each person repeat what the first person was heard to say. This promotes understanding even further. It is not enough just to listen. You must also establish that you have clearly understood the other person.

Only after exchanging views is it then appropriate to talk about possible solutions. When agreement can be reached on a solution, it is equally important to agree that it is a solution "for now." Plans are made to come back and discuss whether mutual satisfaction has been found. Another attempt might even be necessary. Try these stages the next time you are in conflict with someone important to you.

Do you see the vast amount of attention that has to go into the task of reconciliation? For you to be reconciled with someone, no quick and easy techniques are available. To be reconciled means work! And, of course, there must be agreement that the relationship is worth that amount of work.

Again, the stress that comes from anger can best be resolved by careful attention to the broadening of your perceptions. What is the relationship worth to you over the long haul rather than in this tense moment?

Stress and Fatigue

Now we return to your body. One of the greatest sources of stress in life comes from failure to take good care of your body. When you push yourself too hard, your body begins to pay a price. When fatigued, you are under stress, and all the other symptoms that we have been discussing begin to emerge.

Wayne Oates has made the comparison that anger is to hate as being tired is to being fatigued. In other words, anger, if dealt with quickly, consumes less energy and time to bring about reconciliation. If anger is not tended to for a long period of time, we can move to a state of hate, which takes far more time and energy to resolve.

In the same way, when you become tired, it is important that you rest. If you do not do so, you can move into a state of fatigue that will take far longer for recovery.

Discoveries are being made regularly in the field of medicine about the importance of caring for your body. Exercise, which is becoming more and more popular, is showing clear and helpful results. Brief acceleration of heartbeat, assuming that you are in good physical condition, leads to an experience that we often describe as "a second wind" or "getting a high." We now know that with the sustained, brief acceleration of heart rate, your body begins to produce endorphins, which are natural pain relievers. These endorphins raise your pain threshold, and more and more evidence seems to indicate that they also "bleed off" some of the stress that you are undergoing. As your body's chemical balance is changed with the secretion of these endorphins, you in fact get better.

Preventive Maintenance

The illustrations that I have given above include only a few of the areas of stress that you and I face in our daily lives. Such examples, however, serve us well as a base from which to draw some general conclusions about how to deal with stress. Let me list them for you.

First, take care of your body. It is important that you exercise in some way. It is equally important that you listen to your body. There are many occasions when we experience bodily symptoms that are important clues about areas of our lives in which we may be abusing ourselves. Have you ever had a cold or some other kind of illness shortly after finishing a major project that demanded much of your energy? That may in part be a signal from your body that it's time to "conk out" for a while.

I remember several years ago when I had increased the number of working hours for myself. Breaks were rare. After this had gone on for some three months, I began to feel a burning and gnawing sensation in my stomach. My physician confirmed my suspicions. An ulcer was developing. At that point, one part of the treatment included keeping my stomach full. I was not to go for more than a couple of hours without getting something to eat or drink. I chose to avoid taking food and drink with me to work. Every two hours, I would leave my office, take a walk, and nibble awhile. It was important, from my point of view, to see, or perceive, that my body had chosen a symptom to interrupt my stressful behavior. Watch out for the temptation to rely on medication to cure the symptom so that you can ignore the message that your body may be sending you.

Second, it's important to understand stress, look for its

sources, and try to know what is going on. Throughout this book, I have attempted to give you the names of authors whose works may be helpful to you in gaining understanding of yourself, other people, and the kind of situations in which you find yourself. I will provide a bibliography at the end of the book to assist you further. "Understanding" is a vehicle for gaining a sense of stability. One of your marvelous characteristics as a human being is your capacity to feel in control of something simply by understanding it. The stories of some persons in traumatic situations like the death camps of Germany during World War II are testimony to the power of the mind to preserve sanity when everything seems insane and out of control. Find some helpful frame of reference that enables you to understand not only what you are doing but why you are doing it.

As a third resource for dealing with stress, diversify your gratification. Don't become so focused on your work, for instance, that you develop no other interests. A hobby, or even multiple hobbies, can provide important diversion and enjoyment. Sometimes you become so focused on one relationship that you fail to cultivate other friends. You need more than one relationship in your life. There may even be times in which that person is no longer available to you. There should be other relationships to which you can turn for support.

A fourth resource for dealing with stress involves giving up. We do need to acknowledge our limits. Some things simply cannot be controlled or even understood. In such times, thrust yourself into God's care. Giving up can be a true resource for you. You can even breathe a sigh of relief when you acknowledge that you cannot take responsibility for some things.

Fifth, learn to share your burdens. You have different

options for sharing your load with others. Share with whoever comes down the hall next! Or be more selective. Whatever your style of sharing, trust it. But please use it. You were not designed to live in isolation. You are God's creature, born to live in community. Cultivate your capacity to live in community. It doesn't come automatically. You keep on learning.

And that leads to the sixth resource for dealing with stress: Realize that stress itself can be a learning experience. Stress is a reminder of your limits. Some situations press in and demand that you pay attention to them. If you fight them or run away, you really do not grow. Stress is an invitation for a leap of faith. When you are under stress, recognize that you are on the verge of learning something. That realization alone can excite you about expanding your perception. The alternative is to narrow it out of desperation.

Stress is a powerful force in life. It reminds you that you are human. Let me remind you that you are not alone. Stress also reminds you that you are a creature of possibility. Broaden your perception and understanding of stress. It will provide you with much power—power within yourself, and power that is available from God.

Part III

THE POWER OF YOUR PERCEPTIONS

Chapter 8

Perception and Growth

I have described one way of understanding our nature as human beings in the early chapters of this book. Then I discussed the effects of perception on the way we deal with some of our problems in living. Please don't assume that all our perception-changing is directed toward some desperate attempt to correct already existing problems. That is not the case.

An equally important value in understanding perception and learning about yourself has to do with growth. Don't get me wrong. I'm not about to launch you off into another wide-eyed, overly optimistic chase after perfection. I'm talking about growth as a child of God.

Remember that I talked about the importance of understanding your assumptions about human nature. I attempted to set forth a basic description that comes from a religious perspective. Those characteristics included an acknowledgment of our finitude and our way of distorting things in our favor. At the same time, we acknowledged some genuine gifts and sources of richness that were available to us.

Other perspectives about human nature tend to overplay either the finitude and sin or the giftedness. We have been trying to walk with a delicate balance that carries integrity.

A proper understanding of who you are can help to expand your perception to an awareness of just how much power you have and can also expand the relative understanding of your limits. This chapter will talk about some of the areas to which you need to give attention for responsible growth.

Commitment

The very first element in launching a program of growth involves knowing where you stand. Commitment is my preferred word to describe "taking a stand." It is very difficult for you to go anywhere if you don't know where you are now.

In one sense, commitment involves pledging yourself to a set of values. Practically all religious groups have some kind of confession of faith, to which they ask all members to commit themselves. Those confessions of faith are attempts to put into words certain commonly held beliefs and assumptions. The writers of those confessions, many of which date back thousands of years, knew the importance of commitment.

In your own growth, it is important for you to examine your commitments. You may discover that you really don't understand the commitments that you have made religiously, or you may not have made any commitments at all. Look about you, though, at the commitments that exist in your life. If you are married, you have committed yourself to some vows. If you work, there are certain standards of excellence that you have agreed to maintain. In friendships, there is a mutual understanding (which may or may not have been spoken out loud) to which both of you hold. If you are a parent, you have committed yourself to certain standards by which you will raise your children. When those standards are uncertain or become hazy, consequences are paid by both the children and you the parent.

So, commitment deserves your early and regular attention. Take some time to look at the values that are most important to you. What sort of relationships are you striving for and want to encourage others to value? What sort of world, government, leadership, etc., are you willing to work for? Believe it or not, these kinds of commitments have a great deal of impact on how you deal with more personal issues.

To take a look at your commitments is to expand your perception. When you begin to make the things that are important to you "speakable," you find yourself having greater influence on where you go from there. As Bandler and Grinder describe it, the more you verbalize your agreements, the more you gain an understanding of your "deep structure" (*The Structure of Magic*). As you examine and expand that "deep structure," there is more power available to you for decision-making and growth.

Teachability

If I simply stopped with a discussion of commitment, I might find that I have encouraged a great deal of stubbornness. Most of us, when pushed, will make strong declarations about what we believe and what we stand for. The trouble is that we seldom are willing to examine those commitments.

Resistance to examining our standards is understandable. After all, if we look at them too closely, we might have to change them. Of course, that's what growth is all about. Teachability means that we are willing to learn something new, even if the things that we learn call us to reform some of our commitments.

Remember that in our discussion of human nature we

emphasized our human resistance to change. In fact, one of the ways that I like to describe sin is as a preference for remaining miserable in a familiar way, rather than go through the inconvenience of changing ourselves!

That's your temptation if you think that you have all the answers. Teachability is essential because of the very fact that we are limited creatures. You cannot know everything! Therefore, it is important for you to read, discuss, share, and find other vehicles for observation, listening, thinking, and feeling to help expand your horizons. In the next chapter I will suggest some resources for developing your teachability.

Acknowledgment of Limits

Yes, that's right. I want you to take a look at your short-comings. Skewed perception is very good at helping you avoid those shortcomings. But when you don't know your limits, you lose a great deal of potential power. You become trapped by your not knowing.

One of the limitations that I must face time and time again is my inability to say no when my schedule is already full. As I mentioned earlier, I then wind up having to go back later, apologizing, asking forgiveness, staying up late at night, etc. If only I could recognize my limitations more quickly, I would do a great deal better. Fortunately, with reminders from friends and family, and with more determined effort on my part, I have begun to recognize those limits. But I really could not do it alone.

That's one of the ways of working at a better understanding of your limits—getting others to help you. As a limited creature, you cannot get along absolutely by yourself. Find a close friend, a spouse, or some other helper to assist you in doing a close inspection of yourself from time to time. You'll be amazed at how discovery of weakness leads to strength.

Claiming Our Strengths

This section *must* accompany the preceding one. An overemphasis on recognizing your weaknesses can readily cause you grave harm. However, if you also carry out an inspection to claim your strengths, you can begin to focus on the areas where you have the greatest contributions to make.

One of the limits I have slowly come to recognize about myself is that I am not an original thinker. It is true that I teach and write, but those projects in which I have asked myself to come up with new ideas, concepts, etc., have been the most painful times for me.

That recognition of my limits, however, has led me to discover a strength. While I am not an original thinker, I think I am a good translator of other people's thoughts. Consequently, you may have noticed that I frequently refer in my writing to the works of other people. I attempt to summarize them, put them in a different way, and generally be helpful to those who might not otherwise read the more complicated discussions by these various persons.

It was only after I recognized my limits that I could really recognize and develop my strengths. By not often demanding of myself that I write a *new* book, I can now devote myself more willingly and energetically to tasks that are my cup of tea.

Take some time to look at your gifts. Have you been demanding things of yourself that really just don't seem to fit? What are the real strengths and contributions you see yourself to have? Think about—and talk with someone else

about—the ways in which you might develop those gifts more
fully.

Being Valued

One of the essential ingredients for growth is a sense of
being valued. All of us need to know that we matter to
someone else, but we do not always have very effective ways
of confirming that.

Growing up as a Southerner trained me well in not
accepting compliments. After all, accepting compliments and
even agreeing with them was a sign of pride! Pride has always
been labeled a bad thing in my culture. Therefore, I learned
to translate all compliments into something to be denied. You
may experience it yourself, or you may have seen another
person do it—upon receiving compliments, he or she looks at
the floor and says, "Oh, it really wasn't anything."

While that may be good manners, we can translate it, if we
take it too seriously, into saying that we ourselves are not
anything. If we are really going to expand our perception in
the ways already described above, we have to be willing to
claim both our limitations and our gifts. Then we can be
thankful when people tell us what they value in us, rather
than pretend that they are wrong. Take some time to cultivate
relationships where honest exchange of appreciation and
affection can take place. Each of us needs to receive and give
such gifts.

Power

The items I have listed above may seem fairly obvious to
you. In fact, you may wonder why I bothered to list them at
all. However, I would be very surprised if there were not one

or two that you found yourself neglecting, even if you were already familiar with their importance.

Power, as we have talked about it, is a strange thing. Different from physical strength and political or economic power, this particular kind of power is much more closely tied to your ability to cope with things. It is a kind of power that deals with much more basic survival.

We may be rich. We may have great influence. We may even have big muscles! But if we do not have an internal sense about our ability to cope, we are very weak indeed. In fact, many people who accumulate wealth, political power, brute strength, and various kinds of IOU's are often compensating in some way for their internal sense of vulnerability.

This power involves a sense of confidence that accompanies us during our moments of perceived weakness. A very difficult concept to describe, perhaps it can best be understood as a genuine sense of assurance that we have a variety of options at our disposal during hard times.

The greatest sense of weakness you may feel is that of having only one option at your disposal. To have only one survival strategy certainly leaves a person with a sense of panic. *Everything* rides on that one plan! When your perception expands to the point where many options are seen and they are not even limited to your own abilities, then you have some sense of a "greater power."

A growing sense of that power is the norm. We never "get it." It is always something that is developing, sometimes expanding and sometimes shrinking. If we can accept that reality about ourselves as well, then we are indeed people of faith and expanding awareness.

Chapter 9

Back to the Beginning: The Source and Wisdom of Your Power

I believe that you and I are children of God. This book seeks to help you perceive more of what that belief means. Part of being a child of God means that you have been given the power to understand more and more about the precious gifts of being human.

One of those gifts is the power of your perception. And it really is a power! Power can be misunderstood, abused, ignored, or not even recognized. On the other hand, it can be recognized, examined for its possibilities, then used with care and a sense of responsibility. In this chapter I want to foster that kind of spirit—a spirit that moves you to live out the high regard that God has shown for you in giving you the power of perception.

Perception Is a Gift—With Limits

Perception, insight, discovery, discernment, realization, knowing—all these words refer to the agony and the ecstasy of our special characteristics as human beings. We have the ability to see into things, to examine and study and turn things over in our minds. As a result, we can accomplish a great deal. By the same token, we can create a lot of trouble.

In a special relationship with a friend, an associate, or a family member, we can see what is happening before the other person tells us. But sometimes we see something that really isn't happening. The trouble is that we may refuse to acknowledge the distortion on our part:

"You're upset with me!"

"No, I'm not!"

"Yes, you are. I can tell it by the way you looked at me when you walked into the room."

"Look. Nothing is wrong. I'm tired. It's been a hard day. But I'm not mad at you."

"Don't try to conceal it. You're mad. I can see it written all over you."

"Well, I'm certainly starting to get mad now—what with you trying to read my mind all the time."

That conversation, if we can call it that, comes as a result of our perception and its limits. It has been so from the beginning.

The first three chapters of Genesis tell us the story about ourselves. And the story continues with infinite versions. God creates human beings in his image, with his likeness and with dominion over the earth (Gen. 1:26–31). Seeing all creation to be good, as he intended it, God gives Eden to the human beings, and also gives a warning: "But of the tree of the knowledge of good and evil you shall not eat" (Gen. 2:17). Such a temptation! To see and understand everything. It was too much. The warning was passed over. The eyes of the human beings were opened wide. And our struggle with perception was off and running! (Gen. 3). The gift is ours, but at times it is more than we can handle—alone.

Your Limits Have a Purpose

"Why couldn't I handle it?"
"I'd rather do it myself!"
"Look at it from my point of view."

Part of the power of our perception tempts us to think that our point of view is the only one that should count. That's part of the meaning of power—to be in control. Just as we want to win at arm wrestling or draw the prettiest picture, so we want to have the best perception, the keenest insight, or the wittiest joke.

When you work for those purposes, however, another thing happens. You become isolated. To be the first or the "only" is to set yourself apart. And to be set apart may feel good in some moments, but in the long run it hurts. The hurt is not only your own but that of those close to you. So the power has its limitations. That is a painful discovery to make.

One of the most helpful illustrations of this power that isolates is in the book *Celebrate the Sun,* by James J. Kavanaugh. It is the story of a bird named Harry Langendorff Pelican. This is a bird book that contains far more reality and truth than *Jonathan Livingston Seagull* could ever offer! Harry L. wants to surpass all his pelican community. He goes off to learn how to soar with more grace, develop more wisdom, and generally become a hero. The trouble is that he keeps missing out on important events. Tragedies and celebrations pass him by. Some, such as the death of his child, occur in the very midst of his attempts to encourage the spirit of competition. Finally he perceives the isolation he has created for himself and becomes a pursuer of community.

That is what you must watch for in the power of your perception. Don't ignore the finitude, the limits, which were discussed in the first section of this book. To ignore the limits, to claim too much power for yourself, can leave you in a condition that is inhuman. It is a condition that can separate you from other people and from God. The smugness you may feel for a time turns into a trap.

With other human beings, your separation may be evident in an unwillingness to cooperate or consult with others. In your relationship with God, your separation can express itself in a refusal to depend—or the distorted perception that you do not *need* to depend—on the power of the Holy Spirit, from whence your power of perception comes.

The Genesis story makes clear the limitations set on us by God. And there are fascinating places in Scripture that reinforce the reality of those limits. Look with me at Isa. 6:9–10.

> And he said, "Go, and say to this people:
> 'Hear and hear, but do not understand;
> see and see, but do not perceive.'
> Make the heart of this people fat,
>   and their ears heavy,
>   and shut their eyes;
> lest they see with their eyes,
>   and hear with their ears,
> and understand with their hearts,
>   and turn and be healed."

The words clearly direct that people be prevented from perceiving what is going on. Does God deliberately block our perception? Seemingly so. In Exodus, for another example, we are told that *God* hardens Pharaoh's heart. In fact, the Pharaoh is not *allowed* to see what God is doing (Ex. 7:3–4). In the New Testament as well, we can find examples of God's placing specific limits on perception:

> But while they were all marveling at everything he
> did, he said to his disciples, "Let these words sink
> into your ears; for the Son of man is to be
> delivered into the hands of men." But they did not
> understand this saying, and it was concealed from
> them, that they should not perceive it; and they
> were afraid to ask him about this saying. (Luke
> 9:43b–45)

Concealed so that they could not perceive? Yes, and you can
find our Isaiah passage quoted at least twice in the New
Testament, reaffirming limits on the power to perceive. To
what end? Doesn't it seem strange, if not cruel, for God to
limit us in such a way?

Not if you look at the *effects* of that limitation. Those
controls occur at points in the story of God's relationship with
us when we (1) need to acknowledge *God's* power and (2)
need to reaffirm our need for each other—for community.

Had Pharaoh's heart not been hardened, had he simply
said, "Nice idea, Moses, take them away," there would have
been no occasion for Israelites or Egyptians to see and
acknowledge the power of God. Had the disciples immediately seen the agony that lay before them, they might well
have panicked and run. Thank God we *don't* know everything
in advance. Thank God for the Holy Spirit that works in us to
use us in ways that we cannot anticipate. Thank God for those
moments when we realize we don't have all the power and can
lean on him and each other. (I am indebted to the biblical
scholar James Sanders for some of my thinking on this, and
will recommend a book of his in the last chapter of this book.)

Your Limits in Perception Place You in God's Hands

God's marvelous ways of bringing us into contact with our
limits can be painful moments in our lives. But those mo-

ments also offer us the opportunity to perceive and experience the reality of God's grace. In Chapter 4, I talked about suffering. Times of suffering are often times when we feel out of control, when we can't get things to go the way we planned. They *may* be moments, however, when we have to acknowledge God's power. As long as we can be in control, we don't really have to confess that we have our limits.

Have you ever had a time in which you just didn't know what to do? I can't imagine anyone's not having had such a time. Not only did you not know what was best, but neither did anyone else. Perhaps it was a decision about whether to marry. Maybe you wrestled with a decision about placing a parent in a nursing home. Should you have joined in a stand taken by the church about racial injustice? Even the hesitation about giving food or money to a beggar on the street was a moment when you just didn't really know what you ought to do. And then, you decided something. You did something. But there was a trust implicit in that moment. You were trusting that you did the right thing even though you didn't know for sure.

I am not claiming that when you made such a decision you placed yourself in God's hands. You certainly were having to admit that you didn't really know what was best. At the very least, however, you acknowledged that you just didn't know enough to be really in charge.

That kind of realization can be a first step toward placing yourself in God's hands. It is the *perception* that power beyond your own is needed in a situation. That very perception, which is our gift, has the power to help us see our limitations and give us a sense of vision about where to turn.

Your perception enables you to see that you are in God's hands. The power in that perception enables you to place yourself willingly in God's hands. You are enabled to do so by the very limitations that you are able to recognize. To come to that realization can be a prayerful moment. In fact, the prayer of Paul in Rom. 8:26–27 is a beautiful expression of the truth that is contained in such moments:

> Likewise the Spirit helps us in our weakness; for we do not know how to pray as we ought, but the Spirit himself intercedes for us with sighs too deep for words. And he who searches the hearts of men knows what is the mind of the Spirit, because the Spirit intercedes for the saints according to the will of God.

Our weakness and inability are acknowledged—"we do not know how." Yet the Spirit is there, waiting, available. Our place is in God's hands. We are those saints for whom God waits and cares. Thank God for the perception that enables us to know it.

Your Limits in Perception Push You Into Community

Being placed in God's hands is one of the gifts of having only limited perception. A further gift is that of community. We are forced to rely on each other. Since our perception is not enough, God gives us the perception of others who see things differently. While that is a gift, we may turn it into a problem if we fall back on our temptation to be self-reliant. That is why I have used the word "pushed" in the title of this section. There are moments when we don't want to see things another way, but reality and God's grace often force us to do so.

The perception of other people enables us to see when we have been wrong, but that is a two-edged sword. We can be wrong in more than one way. One wrong may be what we have often called the sin of pride. It is our certainty that we are always right, and others had better sit up and take note. The old line, "I've only been wrong once in my life and that was when I thought I was wrong and turned out to be right," is a beautiful illustration of that kind of wrong.

Another kind of misperception, however, is one that fails to recognize the very gifts that we have. We may have ignored or denied them. One of the joys in my work is to see the reactions of persons when someone helps them to see abilities that had lain dormant for years, unrecognized.

One of the powers of perception, then, is to enable others to see things about themselves that they had never recognized or acknowledged. Perception can make things "speakable" between people. And once the gifts or the wrongs have been identified, then people can work *together* to grow as a result of what they have seen and acknowledged.

Scripture itself is a record of and by the community of faith, not just of one individual. Scripture, too, is a gift to the community of faith, assuring that the perceptions continue and are understood more clearly. Some examples from Scripture may help.

> Ever since the creation of the world his invisible nature, namely, his eternal power and deity, *has been clearly perceived* in the things that have been made (Rom. 1:20, italics added)

> When you read this *you can perceive* my insight into the mystery of Christ (Eph. 3:4, italics added)

> *When they saw* that I had been entrusted with the gospel ... and *when they perceived* the grace that was given to me ... [they] gave to me and Barnabas the right hand of fellowship, that we should go ... (Gal. 2:7, 9, italics added)

Notice the characteristic use of perception in those illustrative verses: Insight is shared with a community in order to come to a shared understanding. *Perception is far more a gift to community than it is a gift to an individual.*

In the work of counseling, I have come more and more to the understanding that one person cannot tell you how it is. That one person doesn't know! The only way to come to a deeper understanding of what is going on in people's lives is by inquiring into the community's shared wisdom about what is going on. *All* members of a family need to be consulted! The system has a perception that is far wiser than the perception of any one person.

> But grace was given to each of us according to the measure of Christ's gift. . . . And his gifts were that some should be apostles, some prophets, . . . to equip the saints for the work of ministry, for building up the body of Christ (Eph. 4:7, 11–12).

You have a gift. You can perceive things from a point of view that is uniquely yours. That gift has power. It can shape decisions and perceptions of other people. You contribute to your family and to the community of faith by sharing that gift. As you understand the power that comes from sharing it, not only the perception of the community will be increased, but the very decisions of the community will be strengthened. Remember that the gift is not yours alone. It is a gift to community. I hope that you will willingly be pushed into the community as you recognize the power that is yours.

In the Hands of God and Community, You Have the True Power of Perception

Recognizing that you are limited and dependent on God's grace gives you strength. Becoming a part of a community, rather than standing over against it, gives you strength. That is one of the strange paradoxes of the Christian faith. Whether it makes sense or not, it is true.

A large part of the power of perception is not your own. It is a gift from God. Thus, changing your perception or coming to terms with difficult areas of your life does not depend on your power alone. Power is there, even when you do not see it. The power is yours to see things through another's eyes. The power is yours to make decisions on the basis of others' wisdom. The power is yours to rely on others' strengths and perceptions when your own fail. The power is yours to rely on God's mercy even when all seems hopeless.

Changing your perception and salvaging a tough situation is not just up to you. The responsibility and insight are distributed. Although you can't expect God or other people to rush in and magically straighten out your difficulties or dance with you in your moments of joy, neither do you have to agonize or dance alone. That is what the power of perception is: a realization that you are not alone and that multiple powers of caring and mercy are there for you. What are some of those powers?

You have the power to perceive what other people mean. You can clarify and ask for explanation. You can invite other people's insights and wisdom about your own decisions. You can even gain some understanding just by observing people and using your common sense about human nature. Experience is a wonderful teacher, but your perception needs always to be checked against others' perceptions.

You have the power to assert your own perceptions. There are moments when you have important contributions to make for the well-being of other people. They need to hear your insight and will benefit from it. Your participation in their lives becomes an important and responsible way of being in community. And it helps to create a context in which they will trust you with their own perceptions. They will see that you see the value of their gifts of perception as well.

You have the power to perceive yourself more clearly. Through the perceptions of the community, the knowledge of God's design for human beings, the contributions of research and common knowledge and through your own observations, you can understand what "makes you tick." That insight frees and empowers you to make changes within the limits we discussed earlier.

You have the power to pray. Because you are in God's hands, there is always the resource of knowingly cooperating with his intention for all of us. Called to have dominion, we are still his children. And as his children, we can and should call on him in all times and circumstances and benefit from and seek to cooperate with his will.

Take advantage of the power that is yours. It is your gift. And it comes to you in the perfect package—God's grace and the human community. My prayer for you and for myself in the use of this power is best expressed in the words of Paul:

> And it is my prayer that your love may abound more and more, with knowledge and all *discernment,* so that you may approve what is excellent, and may be pure and blameless for the day of Christ, filled with the fruits of righteousness which come through Jesus Christ, to the glory and praise of God. (Phil. 1:9–11, italics added)

Chapter 10

Suggestions for Further Reading

As I have mentioned in Chapter 8, I view myself as a translator of other people's ideas. Many references have been made to other writers and works in the process of writing this book. This last chapter is aimed at acquainting you with some of these resources to which you may want to turn in further developing your own sense of perception and power.

For reading that deals in more depth with personality and human nature, there are several books that I would recommend. *Neurosis and Treatment: A Holistic Theory* by András Angyal, edited by E. Hanfmann and R. M. Jones (John Wiley & Sons, 1965), is still one that I find helpful for a fundamental understanding of human nature. Angyal describes us as constantly dealing with the tension between the need to be autonomous (independent) and homonomous (dependent). His discussion of personality in these terms in the first half of that book is very helpful, though it is sometimes technical.

To work at the understanding of human nature from a theological perspective, a very helpful little book is *Man: Christian Anthropology in the Conflicts of the Present* (Fortress Press, 1974), by Jürgen Moltmann. In the first few pages of that book, Moltmann provides us with a fairly brief but helpful description of who we are as human beings and then moves on to some of the implications to be drawn from his thought.

Easier reading can be found in *Please Understand Me,* by David Keirsey and Marilyn Bates (Prometheus Nemesis Book Co., 1978). They provide a helpful brief personality inventory at the front of the book which is based on the Myers-Briggs Type Indicator. Whether you take the inventory or not, their discussion of some of the genetic predispositions that we have as human beings is helpful and delightful reading.

To build on the work of Keirsey and Bates, I would recommend *Gifts Differing,* by Isabel Briggs Myers and Peter B. Myers (Consulting Psychologists Press, 1980). In fact, Keirsey and Bates have built on the Myerses' studies, but their writing is probably a better starting point. *Gifts Differing* can be more easily understood, I think, after one gets the more basic orientation to the concepts that Keirsey and Bates provide.

For reading that deals more specifically with perception, I would recommend *Stations of the Mind,* by William Glasser (Harper & Row, 1981). Known primarily for his development of "reality therapy," Glasser has become intrigued by the studies of the brain that have been done in recent years. In this book, he develops a careful model for understanding perception that makes for fascinating reading.

Moving on from Glasser to specific understanding of stress and ways of coping with it, I would recommend two books. The more easily read one is *The Road Less Traveled: A New Psychology of Love, Traditional Values and Spiritual Growth* (Simon & Schuster, 1978), by M. Scott Peck. Peck is a psychiatrist who has a gift for writing understandably. The early parts of the book are by far the more helpful ones, as he takes a very realistic view of living in our times.

A more technical book is *The Stress of Life,* by Hans Selye (rev. ed., McGraw-Hill Book Co., 1978). Selye is known as the "guru" on stress. His work was carried out with great care, and his findings have been helpful to many other investigators and counselors working with people who have been overcome by their own stress in life.

I referred earlier in this book to the work by Richard Bandler and John Grinder, *The Structure of Magic,* Volumes I and II (Science & Behavior Books, 1975, 1976). These books provide an amazing insight into the function and power of language. While they are written from a very therapeutic perspective, you might find some cursory reading, of the first volume in particular, enlightening to you about your own language and how it expands or narrows your perception.

Recovery from a broken relationship is a difficult task at best, whether the break is a result of death, separation, or divorce. Bruce Fisher has written a very helpful little book entitled *Rebuilding: When Your Relationship Ends* (San Luis Obispo, Calif.: Impact Publications, 1981). His insight into the stages of seeing yourself and your possibilities from a new perspective is valuable.

When a marital relationship is broken by divorce, children face the recovery process, too. Richard Gardner has provided a valuable resource for younger children in his book *The Boys and Girls Book About Divorce* (Bantam Books, 1971). Since then, he has added to his helpful work by publishing *The Parents Book About Divorce* (Bantam Books, 1979). Teenagers have their struggles also when their parents divorce. They need a book with a bit more sophistication than Gardner's. For them I recommend my own book, *When Your Parents Divorce* (Westminster Press, 1980). All these books recognize the importance of attitude or perspective in the recovery process and provide helpful tools for working toward growth in the best sense of the word.

Grief is a part of the separation and divorce issue discussed above. But grief is by no means confined to divorce or death. Recognizing the broader dimensions of grief and the uniqueness of each of us, Wayne Oates has published *Your Particular Grief* (Westminster Press, 1981) as a ministry to each of us as we move through times of loss in our lives.

Family life is a dimension of our living that calls for broad and changing perceptions almost daily. Each family member is going through his or her own developmental stages. Yet the preservation of a sense of unity and caring has its own continuing demands. Virginia Satir has been helpful in this area for a long time. Perhaps her book *Peoplemaking* (Science & Behavior Books, 1972) is still the best one to read first. The wealth of her perspective lies in her perception that family health is most likely when each member gives equal attention to self, to the other members of the family, and to the best "rules" for living together.

Sometimes our own sense of wrongdoing can narrow our perception in crippling ways. While guilt is an important part of our emotional and spiritual makeup, it can become distorted and leave us feeling isolated and afraid. Two books that have been around for a long time still continue to offer a ministry to us in such times. Lewis Sherrill's *Guilt and Redemption* (rev. ed., John Knox Press, 1957) and Paul Tournier's *Guilt and Grace* (Harper & Row, 1962) should not be ignored. Their understanding of what we human beings are like, combined with their clear belief in God's forgiveness, will bring the power of perception into clear relief for you.

Sometimes reading and hearing about someone else's life

becomes one of our richest sources of encouragement. Such a book is Frederick Buechner's *The Sacred Journey* (Harper & Row, 1982). I heard him deliver the lectures that later were published as this book. There have been few times when I have been so moved and at the same time have learned so much about myself. The power of perception cannot be missed in this man's wisdom and what it can do to give you insight about yourself. He is an author you should not miss.

Autobiography in another form is to be found in Wayne Oates's *Confessions of a Workaholic* (Abingdon Press, 1978). A combination of self-revelation and scholarly insight, the book helps you to look at the existence you live and to reexamine your priorities.

Earlier in this book I expressed appreciation to James Sanders for his insight into the limits of our perception. His ideas helped me to gain insight beyond my own limits during the writing of this book. His own book, *God Has a Story Too* (Fortress Press, 1979), combines good sermons and biblical insight that will strengthen your own understanding of the power and grace that come from living in God's hands. You know more of what those hands are like after reading this book.

My suggestions could go on for much longer. However, I think this is certainly enough initial guidance to help you in your own pilgrimage to greater perception and appreciation for being the fearful and wonderful creature that God has made you. My best wishes to you in your journey—and may it be a journey that is not made alone. Take full advantage of God's presence and the presence of your community, who can share the pathway with you.

Questions for Thought and Discussion

Part I. Understanding Your Perceptions

1. What are some of the characteristics that we all share as human beings?

2. Give some illustrations of your finitude, your sinfulness, and your gifts. Find illustrations that you have in common with other members of your discussion group or your family or friends.

3. Do you believe that we are born with some characteristics that can't be changed?

4. What are some of your characteristics that have been influenced by important people or experiences in your life?

5. What are some of the beliefs that you hold most dear? How do they affect your daily life?

6. What does thinking about these questions do to you? Does this kind of self-examination help you understand yourself and other people any differently?

Part II. Changing Your Perceptions

1. Try to think about some things that you once believed were true that have turned out otherwise. How did you

discover that things were different from what you had first thought?

2. How hard is it for someone to change your mind about something? Talk with friends and see if they agree with you on how hard or easy it is for you to change your mind.

3. Think about a regular stress point in your life now. What are some of the suggestions in this book that might help you in dealing with it?

Part III. The Power of Your Perceptions

1. When are you willing to let someone else or God play a part in your decision-making?

2. How would you describe some of the powers that you have because of your perception?

3. Think of times when:

> your perception seemed to help someone;
> someone else's perception helped you;
> you were aware that you were helpless;
> you experienced God's power.

4. What are some things you can do to strengthen your own reliance on God's grace?

5. What are some things you can do to strengthen your participation in the community of faith? In your family? In the community of the world in which you live?